Good for Busine

Student's book

Good for Business

An intensive course in business English

Student's book

Mark Fletcher and
Roger Hargreaves

Nelson

Thomas Nelson and Sons Ltd
Nelson House Mayfield Road
Walton-on-Thames Surrey
KT12 5PL UK

51 York Place
Edinburgh
EH1 3JD UK

Thomas Nelson (Hong Kong) Ltd
Toppan Building 10/F
22A Westlands Road
Quarry Bay Hong Kong

Distributed in Australia by

Thomas Nelson Australia
480 La Trobe Street
Melbourne Victoria 3000
and in Sydney, Brisbane, Adelaide and Perth

First published by Harrap Limited 1983
(under ISBN 0-245-53718-X)

Second impression published by Thomas Nelson and Sons Ltd 1986
ISBN 0-17-444185-1
NPN 9 8 7 6 5
Printed in Hong Kong

Note All the characters and incidents in this book are entirely fictitious and bear no relation, whatsoever to any known person or persons.

Acknowledgements

The authors would like to thank Portex Ltd, manufacturers of medical equipment, for their co-operation. In particular, special thanks are due to Volker Bertram, East European representative for that company, who has acted as consultant on technical and business matters. His very practical comments have been of great help.

The authors and publishers are grateful to the following for permission to reproduce the illustrations:
P Harrison, pp 1, 38; Janine Wiedel, p 17; Cedok (London) Ltd, p 30; Portex Ltd, pp 39, 42, 44, 47, 52; Stephen F Morley, p 42; Port of Liverpool Authority, p 62; Camera Press Ltd (photograph by Jon Blau), p 65; Inbel, p 75; the Hong Kong Government Office, p 82; the British Tourist Authority, p 86; the Automobile Association, p 97.

We should also like to thank the following for permission to reproduce copyright material:
The Automobile Association for the extract on vehicle security from its Motoring Abroad brochure (pp 97–98).
The National Westminster Bank plc for the extract from their publicity material 'Why should I have an Access card?' (p 45).

Contents

Unit 1

Structure:	Present perfect
Functional areas:	Talking about jobs Introductions

Section A Dialogue and language work

A1 Guided listening

Read these questions before you listen to the story. Make notes of the answers while you are listening.

1 What is Chris's job?
2 Does he travel a lot in his work?
3 Where does he meet Ingrid?
4 Has she recently been to Africa?
5 Why are they both going to Vienna soon?
6 Why is Mr Denton interested in their conversation?

Dialogue

It is Friday afternoon in the office of Plastech (Kent) Ltd, a manufacturer of medical equipment in south-east England. Chris Telford, an overseas sales representative, is talking to the Export Manager's secretary.

CHRIS: Have you finished those letters, Sally?
SALLY: Yes, I have. I always finish the mail early on Friday, in case there are any last-minute emergencies.

CHRIS: Yes, of course. I'm a bit out of touch with office routine, I'm afraid. I spend most of my time in railway stations and airports.

SALLY: Go on, you know you enjoy travelling. So what is it this weekend? Golf and good living?

CHRIS: Oh, I don't play much golf these days, I've only played two or three times this year. But I'm going out to dinner at the Pilgrims' House tonight, and tomorrow I've got an invitation to a rather grand party in Chelsea.

SALLY: That sounds fun. I've never been to the Pilgrims' House. Do you recommend it ...?

(Later, in Chelsea. The doorbell rings.)

TONY: Chris! Come in! I haven't seen you for ages! Let me take your coat. Have a drink. How are you?

CHRIS: Oh, I'm fine, thanks. I say, Tony, this place is rather splendid.

TONY: Oh, well, you know how it is in the film business. Up one minute, down the next. And tell me, what do you do now?

CHRIS: I'm a salesman. I sell medical equipment for Plastech, down in Kent.

TONY: Medical equipment? You mean stethoscopes, and sticking plaster, and that sort of thing?

CHRIS: Well, not really, I ...

TONY: Then you must meet Ingrid Fowler. She's a doctor, International Health something, she might even buy something. Ingrid! Ingrid! I say, Ingrid, this is Chris Telford, a very old friend of mine, interested in medicine, and health and so on.

CHRIS: How do you do? Ingrid Fallow, was it?

TONY: Do help yourselves to food when you're ready, won't you? It's through there.

INGRID: Thanks, Tony. Fowler, actually, F-O-W-L-E-R. Quite a party, isn't it?

CHRIS: Oh, Tony always gives good parties, he always has. He knows everybody. Have you known him long?

INGRID: No, I've only just met him.

CHRIS: Look, excuse me, but I haven't got a drink yet. Can I get you another one?

INGRID: Thanks. White wine, please.

CHRIS: Tony tells me you're a doctor.

INGRID: Yes. I'm with the International Health Agency.

CHRIS: Oh, I've heard a lot about them. The work must be very interesting. Do you work overseas?

INGRID: Yes, mainly. I've just come back from six months in Nigeria.

CHRIS: Do you specialize in a particular field?

INGRID: Well, my main interest is in diseases that are carried in water, but it also involves me in general problems about water supply. I'm giving a talk about it next month.

CHRIS: Where?

INGRID: In Vienna. There's an international conference.

CHRIS: Really? That's a coincidence. I shall be there as well.

INGRID: Oh? Are you a medical man, too?

CHRIS: Oh no. At least, I'm not a doctor. I sell hospital equipment, surgical products, catheters and so on.

NEW VOICE: That sounds interesting—I'm in medicine myself.

CHRIS: Oh really? What do you do?

VOICE: Well, let me introduce myself. My name's Laurie Denton. I'm a surgeon at King's Hospital.

CHRIS: I'm Chris Telford, and this is Dr Ingrid Fowler.

DENTON: Pleased to meet you.

INGRID: How do you do?

DENTON: Shall we have a drink together? Dr Fowler, what would you like . . .?

Colloquial terms

out of touch (4) not up to date with the situation
go on (7) used ironically here to mean 'stop pretending'

A2 Focus on structure—Present perfect

1 Has Chris played a lot of golf this year?
2 Tony and Chris don't often meet. How does Tony welcome Chris to the party?
3 Are Tony and Ingrid old friends?
4 Does Ingrid always work in London?

A3 Focus on function—Talking about jobs

1 Tony asks Chris a general question about his job, and gets a general answer. What exactly do they say?
2 Chris asks Ingrid a more detailed question about her job, and gets a more detailed answer. What do they say?

Focus on function—Introductions

3 How does Tony introduce Chris to Ingrid?
4 How does Denton introduce himself, and what do Ingrid and Chris reply?

A4 Vocabulary

Use the story to complete these sentences.

1 Plastech is a ______ of ______ ______.
2 Chris works for them. He is an ______ ______ ______.
3 Sally finishes the letters early on Friday in case there are any ______ ______ ______.
4 Chris doesn't spend much time in the office, so he's ______ ______ ______ with office routine.
5 Tony and Chris haven't seen each other ______ ______.
6 Tony may be an actor, or a director. He works ______ ______ ______ ______.

7 Tony invites them to eat when they are ready. He says, 'Do ______ ______.'

8 Chris wants more details about Ingrid's work. He asks, 'Do you ______ ______ ______ ______ ______?'

9 Two strangers meet in London. They are both going to the same conference in Vienna. What a ______!

10 Denton offers to get Ingrid a drink. '______ ______ ______ ______?'

Section B Extension work—Grammar practice

Present perfect tense

I haven't seen you for ages
Have you known him long?

In the examples above we use the present perfect tense to indicate a length of time, as if answering the question *how long?*—usually with the information **since . . .** (*when*) or **for . . .** (*how long*).

I've just come back from six months in Nigeria
I've never been to the Pilgrims' House

In the examples above we again mention something in the past but we are not interested in the exact time when it happened. We use the present perfect with:

(i) **ever?** (meaning *at any time*?), **already, just, yet**
(ii) expressions which say *how often*, for example, **rarely, sometimes, never, three times**

B1 Fluency practice

Make complete sentences, using the words in brackets.

Example: I / not / much golf this year. (*play*)
I haven't played much golf this year.

1 How long / you / for the IHA? (*work*)
2 I / with them for five years. (*be*)
3 You / ever / Nigeria? (*be*)
4 Yes / three times. (*be*)
5 Chris / Tony a long time? (*know*)
6 Yes, they / each other since university. (*know*)
7 You / the latest sales figures? (*see*)
8 Yes, we / very well. (*do*)
9 You / the telex to Plastech yet? (*send*)
10 No, because I / not / the total order from the Purchasing Department yet. (*have*)

B2 Free stage

Work in pairs. Interview each other to complete this questionnaire.

Ask: *How long have you* (*been in your present job*)*?*
Have you ever . . .?
How often have you . . .? or, *How many times have you . . .?*

	Number of years	Travel/holidays	Yes/No	Number of times
Present job		USA		
Present town		Middle East		
Present accommodation		Skiing holiday		
Present car		Package tour		

Section C Extension work—Functional areas

C1 Talking about jobs

Listen to the extracts from the story on the tape. Note down the phrases and expressions used to talk about jobs. Then prepare and give a short (one-minute) talk about your company and your job. Find any specialized vocabulary you need in a dictionary.

Introductions

Listen to the extracts from the story. Work in groups of three. Introduce the person next to you to another student. You must give more information about the person than just his name. Do this until everyone in the class has met everyone else. Make sure you get the names exactly right.

C2 Consolidation

Complete the conversation below and then practise it with a partner.

KOTERA: May I introduce myself? My name is Kotera.
YOU: ....
KOTERA: I'm from Tokyo. I'm an engineer with Nippon Dynamics.
YOU: ....
KOTERA: Yes, I specialize in thermodynamics; gas turbines in particular.
YOU: ....
KOTERA: I've been here three days, at the Engineering Conference.
YOU: ....
KOTERA: Oh, thank you. I'd like a Scotch and soda, please.

Section D Listening work

D1 Structure exercise—Present perfect

Use the prompts below to help you to answer the questions you will hear on the tape.

Example: How long have you worked for Plastech?
I've worked there for six years.

1 six years
2 Switzerland, Italy, Norway
3 about six months
4 since 9 o'clock
5 since university
6 about three years
7 two films

Now you ask *have you ever* ...? questions.

Example: Question One. Mr Kotera.
Have you ever met Mr Kotera?

1 Mr Kotera (*meet*)
2 the film 'Manhattan' (*see*)
3 America (*be*)
4 Concorde (*fly*)
5 a video tape recorder (*use*)

D2 Story extract—Focus on function

Listen to the extract from the dialogue. Then listen and repeat.

D3 Listening for information

Laurie Denton is asking Chris some questions about his job. Listen to the conversation and complete his notes.

Listen to the tape again and answer the questions about Chris Telford's job.

Now you *ask* the questions. Use Laurie Denton's notes to help you.

1. Company-name?
2. Address?
3. Products?
4. Specialities?
5. Employees-how many?
6. Chairman-name?
7. Export-biggest customers?
8. Salesmen-how many?

Section E Group work

Talking about jobs

The following expressions are frequently used in describing people's jobs:

He is responsible *to* someone *for* something.
She is in charge of ...
He deals with ...
She is involved in ...
He is required to ...
She is expected to ...

He must be able to . . .
She is in control of . . .
He must have experience of . . . / experience in . . .
She must be qualified in . . . / have qualifications in . . .
He must be qualified as a . . .

Look at the job advertisements here and see how many of these expressions you can find. Write down the sentences containing the expressions.

Calling for entrepreneurial qualities, with scope to become a Divisional Manager in 2-3 years, with considerably increased earnings

SALES PRODUCT MANAGER — OILFIELD EQUIPMENT

DHAHRAN, SAUDI ARABIA US$70,000 – $80,000 net

Oilfields Service Equipment – Worldwide Interests – Sales $150 million

We are inviting applications for this new position from candidates aged 25-35 who are preferably qualified as Mechanical/Petroleum Engineers. They must have experience of oil equipment (4 years minimum) and have at least 2 years experience in selling it. The successful candidate will be required to report to the Divisional Manager in Dhahran and will be responsible for selling down hole tools, rig handling equipment, mud systems and production equipment in Saudi Arabia. He must be able to identify sales opportunities, and will be required to enter into commercial discussions and to agree technical specifications with oilfield engineers. He will be in charge of an experienced sales team and will be expected to carve out a significant share of the market.

Initial salary negotiable in the range US$70,000-$80,000, plus car, provident fund, house, free medical insurance, children's educational allowance and holiday air passages, home leave air passages.

Applications in strict confidence to Managing Director, quoting reference SPM 42/B/82 — MG.

SMITH-RIGBY INTERNATIONAL (Executive Recruitment Consultants)
492 Cannon Street London EC3 6FF Phone 01-668 5728 Telex 965463

The Settlement Association promotes, funds and monitors housing associations. The new South-Western region with offices based in Bristol and Exeter needs an

AREA DIRECTOR

The Area Director is responsible to the Deputy Chief Executive in charge of the Association's development programme. The Director will be involved in policy, strategy and day-to-day implementation and will be in control of the District Managers and their teams which cover the South West.

We seek a successful manager with at least 5 years experience in the housing field plus a degree or appropriate professional qualification, who can expect on appointment a salary of

£17,500 + car

For further details and application forms contact Ian Davidson, Chief Officer Personnel, The Settlement Association, 25 Robin Lane, Bristol BL4 1DR Tel 0272-946-6378 Ext. 411

Settlement SA Association

Development Planning

An Administrative

ASSISTANT/SECRETARY

Salary £6,250 — 7,050 p.a. inc.

is required to work for the Economic Development Officer and to undertake administrative work in the Industrial Development Unit which is concerned with projects aimed at revitalising the local economy.

The successful candidate will have a flexible approach to a wide-ranging workload and must be able to deal tactfully with businessmen at all levels as well as with the general public. He/she should also possess good typing/shorthand/audio skills and have appropriate administrative experience.

For further details telephone Polly Dunhill, Extension 362 at Lyminge Town Hall, Tel. 0303-862599, quoting reference CANU 26/A

Closing date 18th June.

Applications welcomed from registered disabled people.

Job descriptions

Complete these job descriptions, using the expressions you have met in this section.

The Head of Research and Development is directly ______ ______ the Managing Director ______ carrying out research projects, either in the evaluation of existing systems or the development of new products. He is ______ ______ ______ a staff of qualified engineers and technicians and is ______ to equip and maintain a workshop and laboratory. He is ______ ______ discussions with top management about new projects. He must ______ ______ ______ operate within a planned expenditure budget. He must ______ at least 3 years' ______ ______ Research and Development work in a junior capacity. He is of course ______ ______ an engineer, probably with a degree of MSc or higher.

The Production Manager is ______ ______ ______ all stages of production. He ______ ______ to consult closely with the Marketing and Sales Departments about schedules, production requirements and changing demand. He ______ ______ ______ to reach a quick decision in the event of a breakdown or accident which interrupts production, as he is ______ ______ seeing that delays are kept to a minimum. He is ______ ______ ______ the maintenance staff who look after all the machinery. He is ______ in general discussions about working conditions and safety, and he ______ ______ enquiries and complaints from workers and union representatives about things which affect their welfare; so he must be sensitive and skilled in ______ ______ their problems. He need not have formal ______, but he is ______ ______ have wide ______ of factory operation.

Now work in pairs. Write a job description, similar to the above, for
(a) The Personnel Manager
(b) The Managing Director
Compare your descriptions with those of other pairs. Do these jobs differ in different companies? Do they differ in different countries?

Now each pair should write a job description for any job they choose (perhaps a job in a company that at least one of you knows). Read it out to the others and ask them to decide what the name of the job is.

Reminder of key points in Unit 1

Functional areas

Talking about jobs
What do you do?
I'm with the IHA.
I spend most of my time ...
I sell medical equipment for ...
My main interest is in ...
Do you work overseas?
Do you specialize in a particular field?

Introductions
Let me introduce myself.
I'm Chris Telford, and this is ...
How do you do?
Pleased to meet you.
You must meet Ingrid. She's a ...
I haven't seen you for ages.

Structure: Present perfect

—I've just come back from six months in Nigeria.
—Have you known him long?
—I haven't played much golf this year.

Unit 2

Structure:	Present simple/present continuous contrast
Functional areas:	Making suggestions Telephoning

The story so far: Chris Telford has met Dr Ingrid Fowler at a party, and has discovered that they will be at the same conference in Vienna the following month. He also met Laurie Denton, another doctor.

Section A Dialogue and language work

A1 Guided listening

Read these questions before you listen to the story.

1 Why does Chris want to speak to Mr Fibak?
2 Is it a good time for him to visit Czechoslovakia?
3 What is Medipraha?
4 Why does Chris visit Mr Druce?
5 What does he want to discuss with Tom Richardson (the Export Manager)?

Dialogue

(*The telephone rings.*)

OPERATOR: Czech News Agency, good morning. Can I help you?
CHRIS: May I speak to Mr Fibak, please?
OPERATOR: Who's calling?
CHRIS: My name is Telford, from Plastech Ltd, in Kent.
OPERATOR: Hold the line, please ... you're through.
FIBAK: Fibak speaking.
CHRIS: Oh, good morning Mr Fibak, my name is Telford. I met an acquaintance of yours on Saturday, a Mr Lawrence Denton, and he suggested that you might be able to help me.
FIBAK: What can I do for you, Mr Telford?
CHRIS: Well, my company is hoping to do business in Czechoslovakia, and I was wondering if you could give me some information about the present situation there.
FIBAK: What sort of business is it, Mr Telford?
CHRIS: We export surgical goods and hospital equipment. Perhaps I could call in on you for a few minutes some time today?
FIBAK: How about coming at 2 o'clock? Would that be convenient?
CHRIS: Yes, certainly. I look forward to seeing you at two.
FIBAK: Thank you for calling, Mr Telford. Goodbye.

(*Later, at the offices of Czech News Agency*)

CHRIS: ... and so, Mr Fibak, I wonder if you know anyone I can contact personally in Prague?

FIBAK: Well, the Agency in question is called Medipraha, as you know. As it happens I know the Purchasing Manager there. His name's Novotny, Anton Novotny. You should certainly get in touch with him. You must get a visa from the Trade Mission before you go, of course. Why don't you apply for that now? And then I suggest you telex Novotny shortly before you leave.

CHRIS: That's a good idea. Thank you very much, Mr Fibak, you've been very helpful. And in general, you think it's a good time to make an effort?

FIBAK: Indeed I do. Like all governments, our government doesn't often spend money freely, but at the moment they're spending very large sums on the health service. They're planning four new hospitals in Prague alone, and they're modernizing many existing ones. Obviously they buy most things from Comecon, but these days they are buying more and more from the West—especially sophisticated equipment like yours. Are you going to Prague yourself?

CHRIS: Well, actually our Export Manager is scheduled to go, but he may change his plans, for personal reasons. Now, if you could just let me have a few details ...

(*That afternoon, before returning to Head Office in Kent to see Tom Richardson, his Export Manager, Chris calls at the Foreign Branch of his firm's bank in London.*)

CHRIS: Good afternoon, Mr Druce. It's very good of you to see me.

DRUCE: Sit down, Mr Telford. And how is Mr Richardson?

CHRIS: Oh, he's very well, but his wife has been seriously ill. In fact I may have to go to Czechoslovakia in his place, so I wondered if you could bring me up to date.

DRUCE: Well, things are looking up, actually. They want to increase foreign trade in their current Five-Year Plan, so if you can get into the market your prospects should be quite good. For example ...

... well, I hope tnat puts you in the picture.

CHRIS: Yes, indeed. I take it there's normally no difficulty over payment?

DRUCE: No, they're very reliable, once the contract is signed. They usually agree to pay by Letter of Credit, but you might have to agree to a different method, for competitive reasons.

CHRIS: What do you feel about Export Credit Guarantees? Are they necessary?

DRUCE: Well, you don't have to take out an ECG. Only two things are obligatory in exporting from the UK. First, you must receive payment in full within six months; and second, you have to receive payment in a currency convertible into sterling. So, as I said, the Export Credit Guarantee isn't absolutely necessary, but it protects you against things which you can't control, like any insurance policy. My advice would be to take advantage of that.

CREDIT LIMIT APPLICATION

PLEASE COMPLETE IN **BLOCK LETTERS** AND SEND THIS APPLICATION TO YOUR ECGD REGIONAL OFFICE

In respect of firm business or a current enquiry in excess of the discretionary limit

Name and address of INSURED in full			
Guarantee No.	ECGD USE	ECGD Buyer Ref. No. (if known)	Date of application
Full name of Buyer			
Full address of Buyer (including street, town, country)			
Name and address of Buyer's Bankers (omission may delay a decision)			
Goods			
Limit applied for (ie amount likely to owing at any one time) £		Amount of firm order or current enquiry £	Amount of Current Credit Limit (if any) £
Precise Terms of Payment		Is the buyer a subsidiary of or associated with your company?	Have you previously applied for a Credit Limit on this buyer?

FOR USE IN DEPARTMENT ECG 3377/A Rev. 3/80 Received in RO Checked in RO (initials & date) Submitted to U/W 39 911 914 issued		RO CODE **44**
OBTAIN F/I AWAIT		TYPE 39
SOURCE(S)		
AMOUNT £	TERMS	
REMARKS (if any)		
Name and or address of approved buyer if different from opposite		
AMOUNT APPROVED £	U/W DATE	U/W CODE
SUBJECT TO CONDITIONS:		
U/W	RECOMMENDATIONS	
STATUS RECORDS NOTED		

CHRIS: You've been very helpful, Mr Druce. Thank you very much.

DRUCE: My pleasure, Mr Telford. Good afternoon.

(*The telephone rings.*)

OPERATOR: Plastech Ltd, can I help you?

CHRIS: Nancy, it's Chris Telford. Can you give Sally a message for me?

NANCY: Yes, of course.

CHRIS: Can you tell her I'd like to see Mr Richardson first thing tomorrow morning? I've got something very important to talk to him about. Oh, and Nancy, can I dial to Czechoslovakia, to Prague, direct?

NANCY: Yes, I've got a list here somewhere ... the code's 010 42 2, then you dial the number. But you'd better do it through the international operator if you don't speak Czech ...

Colloquial terms

hold the line please (5) wait a moment (on the telephone)
get in touch with (27) contact (somebody)
things are looking up (54) the situation is improving
...*puts you in the picture* (58) ...gives you the necessary background information

A2 Focus on structure—Present simple/present continuous contrast

1 Why is it a good time for Plastech to sell to Czechoslovakia?
2 Where do the Czechs get most of their hospital equipment? Are things changing?

3 What items does your country export to/import from Comecon? Is trade increasing or decreasing?

A3

Focus on function—Making suggestions

1 Fibak gives Chris three pieces of advice regarding Novotny, his visa and his trip to Czechoslovakia. What are his suggestions? What exactly does he say?

Focus on function—Telephoning

2 How does Chris give the operator his name? How does Fibak answer the phone?
3 Chris rings Nancy. What's the code for Prague?

A4

Vocabulary

Use the story to complete these sentences.

1 The operator connects Chris and says, 'You're ______.'
2 Chris wants to visit Fibak in his office. He says, 'Perhaps I could ______ ______ ______ ______ some time today?'
3 I look ______ to ______ you at two o'clock.
4 The Czech Government ______ ______ four new hospitals and they ______ ______ the existing ones.
5 The Czech Government are buying more and more ______ ______ from the West.
6 Richardson, the Export Manager, isn't keen to go to Czechoslovakia for ______ ______.
7 My information's not very recent. Can you bring me ______ ______ ______?
8 The situation is getting better. Things are ______ ______.
9 The currency you receive has to be ______ ______ ______.
10 Chris wants to see Richardson as soon as possible. In fact he'd like to see him ______ ______ ______ ______.

Section B Extension work—Grammar practice

Present simple/present continuous contrast

Our government doesn't often spend money freely, but at the moment they're spending very large sums on the health service

They buy most things from Comecon, but these days they're buying more and more from the West

The contrast between these two tenses is the difference between
(i) things that happen *always, usually, often, every day, sometimes, never*; that is to say, habits, or things that occur more than once: **My father smokes a pipe** (he is a pipe-smoker)

and

(ii) things that are happening *now, at the present time*; things that have started but not finished yet: **It is raining** (now, at this moment)

B1

Fluency practice

Make complete sentences, using the words in brackets.

Example: Chris ______ a phone call to a customer. He ______ twenty or thirty calls a day. (*make*)
Chris is making a phone call to a customer. He makes twenty or thirty calls a day.

1 Sally ______ about a hundred telexes every week. She usually ______ most of them in the morning. She ______ one to Austria at the moment. (*send*)
2 Mr Druce ______ some advice to Chris. He and his colleagues at the bank ______ advice to companies who want to export. (*give*)
3 Fibak ______ a report on the effect of a recent rise in the value of the pound. He ______ reports on many commercial and economic topics. He usually ______ them on Mondays. (*write*)
4 The Czech government ______ four new hospitals. They ______ two of them in the suburbs of Prague. (*build*)
5 Chris ______ for Plastech. At the moment he ______ on a plan to increase exports to Comecon. (*work*)
6 Plastech ______ a good reputation. They ______ a wide range of products. (*have*)

B2

Free stage

Look at the diagrams showing changes in tourist figures. Use the information to make statements about:

(a) the number of people who usually stay in hotels/holiday camps/other places
(b) the type of accommodation people are staying in this year
(c) the areas where people usually take their holidays
(d) the areas where they are having holidays this year
(e) the number of people who usually travel by plane/car/other methods
(f) the transport situation this year

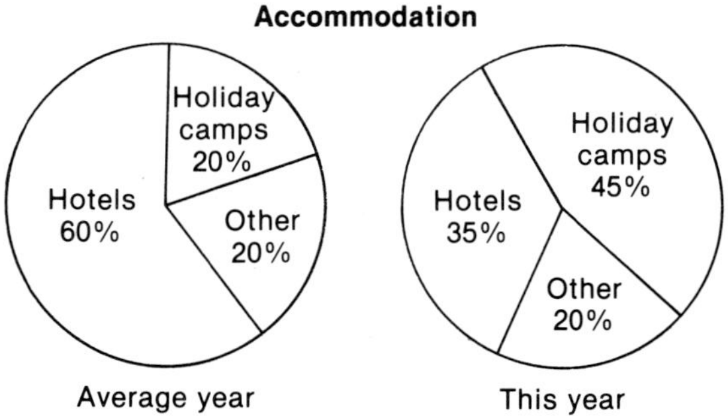

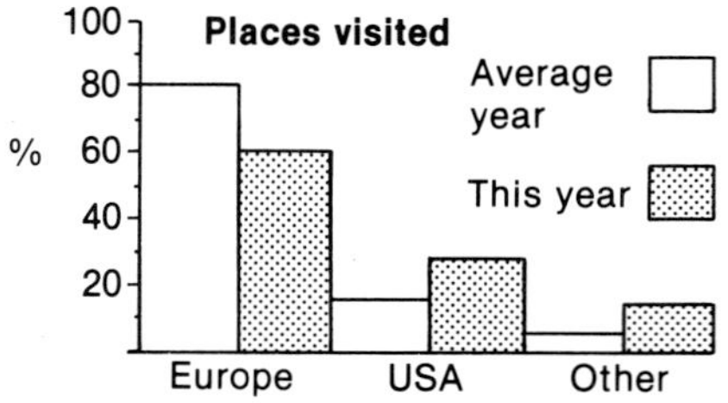

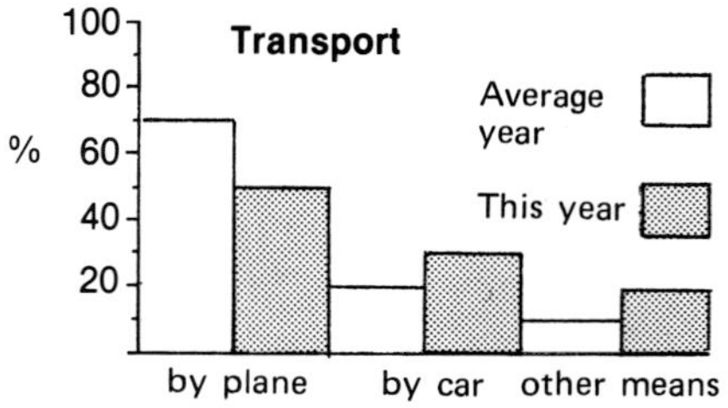

Information about changes in tourist figures

Example: *In an average year 60% of tourists stay in hotels, but this year 35% are staying in hotels.*

Use the information from the diagrams to complete these sentences, using the words in brackets.

1 More people ______ at holiday camps this year than in an average year. (*stay*)
2 About 70% of people usually ______ on holiday by plane. (*go*)
3 Twice as many people ______ a holiday in the USA this year as in an average year. (*have*)
4 What percentage of tourists ______ Europe this year? (*visit*)
5 Tourists usually ______ at hotels. (*stay*)
6 The number of people travelling by car ______ up. (*go*)

Section C Extension work—Functional areas

C1 Making suggestions

In this unit you have seen many ways of making suggestions. Listen to the story on the tape again and complete these suggestions:

FIBAK: How about . . .?
FIBAK: You should . . .
FIBAK: Why don't you . . .?
FIBAK: I suggest you . . . .
DRUCE: My advice would be to . . .
NANCY: You'd better . . .

Now work in pairs, one student taking the part of Chris, the other taking the part of a colleague.

Chris

You are planning your first trip to South America. Ask your colleague, an experienced traveller, about
(a) clothes to take
(b) money—how much? what currencies?
(c) language problems
(d) places to stay
(e) contacts to make before going

Colleague

Answer Chris's questions, using the patterns above to make suggestions.

Using the telephone

Listen again to the telephone conversation between Chris and Fibak. How does Fibak close the conversation?

FIBAK: ....

Now do the exercise below, to practise speaking on the telephone. Work in pairs, one student following the instructions for A, the other for B.

A		B	
1	*Caller*: Call your school and ask for times of classes.	1	*Receptionist*: Provide the information.
2	*Caller*: Call Mr Fibak and ask him for information about Medipraha.	2	*Fibak*: Give the information (including Mr Novotny's name).
3	*Caller*: Call Mr Druce and ask for an appointment.	3	*Druce*: Arrange to see Chris tomorrow (don't forget to ask why, where and when).

C2 Consolidation

A friend is asking you for some information and advice. Complete the conversation and then practise it with a partner.

FRIEND: I want to call a colleague in the States. I've got his name but not his number. What should I do?

YOU: ....

FRIEND: Directory Enquiries? Yes, of course, I'll do that. But how can I make sure that I speak to him in person?

YOU: ....

FRIEND: A person-to-person call ... I see ... Do I have to give my name?

YOU: ....

FRIEND: Yes, I see, so the operator can ring back. Right. Thank you for your help.

YOU: ....

FRIEND: Oh yes, that's a good idea. I'll wait till after 6pm.

Section D Listening work

D1 Structure exercise—Present simple/present continuous contrast

Use the information on tourism on page 14 to answer the questions on the tape.

Example: What proportion of tourists stay in hotels?
Well, in an average year 60% of tourists stay in hotels, but this year 35% are staying in hotels.

D2 Story extract—Focus on function

Listen to the extract from the dialogue. Then listen and repeat.

D3 Listening for information

Mr Druce of the bank is giving Chris some background

information about Czechoslovakia. Take notes on the points below·

Czechoslovakia

1 Area
2 Population
3 Unit of currency
4 Rate of exchange
5 Percentage of trade with Comecon
6 Last Five-Year-Plan—how successful?
7 GNP
8 UK exports to Czechoslovakia
9 UK imports—up or down?
10 Credit facilities—always available?

Use your notes to answer the questions you will now hear on the tape. Then use the points above to *ask* the questions.

Section E Group work

Golden jubilee

Read the following:

In the 1930s, Arthur Kelsall and David Standish started a small market garden business, growing and selling fruit and vegetables. The business did well and has expanded steadily. In the 1950s they diversified into many other activities, all connected with gardening—selling fruit trees, flowering trees, roses, flowers, bulbs, seeds, and designing and selling all kinds of garden equipment, tools, furniture and buildings. There are now three K & S Garden Centres, in Ashford (Kent), Worcester and Lincoln, with an excellent reputation for quality and variety.

Both the founders retired in 1969, and the business is now run by their eldest sons, Thomas Kelsall and Paul Standish, who each have 27% of the share capital. The remaining 46% is held by various members of the family. David Standish died in 1976 but Arthur is still alive and actively interested in the business.

Next year is the 50th anniversary of the founding of the business.

Now work in pairs. You are Thomas Kelsall and Paul Standish, having a telephone conversation. Follow the instructions below.

Thomas Kelsall

Paul Standish

Thomas Kelsall: Ring Paul and suggest that you should organize a special celebration for the firm's Golden Jubilee.

Paul Standish: Agree with Thomas's suggestion. Suggest that you collect ideas on the best way of doing this from as many people as possible.

Thomas Kelsall: Suggest that you consult the family, while Paul contacts the staff.

Paul Standish: Agree. Suggest that everyone should be asked to look for ideas which would be both enjoyable for everyone and good publicity for the firm.

Thomas Kelsall: Suggest that employees should be informed before family members, not after them.

Paul Standish: Agree. Suggest a 'Suggestions Box' for staff at all centres, with a prize for the best idea.

Thomas Kelsall: You think this is a good idea, but suggest that it should be open only to employees, not to the family.

Paul Standish: Agree. Suggest the prize winner should be chosen by a representative of the employees themselves, whom they will elect.

The following week, all employees of K & S, and the members of the two families, received a card like this:

> K&S
>
> *Kelsall & Standish are 50 years old next year! Help us to celebrate this proud occasion in a way which we shall all enjoy, and which will also help to keep us in the public eye.*
>
> *Let us have your suggestions, by post, through the Suggestions Box at your branch, or, better still, by telephoning one of us direct here in Ashford.*
>
> Thomas Kelsall   Paul Standish

Choose three students to play the parts of Thomas, Paul and a secretary.

Stage 1: Suggestions are phoned in to Thomas and Paul alternately, and passed on to the secretary, who makes notes of them all. Your teacher will give you some ideas.

Stage 2: Get together in groups of four. Study the suggestions made (the secretary will give you a list). Suggest ways of improving the ideas that have been put forward, and make further suggestions of your own.

Stage 3: In the same groups, choose what *you* would do for the firm. Tell your teacher and the rest of the class what you have decided. The teacher may ask for a written report.

Reminder of key points in Unit 2

Functional areas

Making suggestions
How about ...?
You should ...
Why don't you ...?
I suggest you ...
My advice would be to ...
You'd better ...

Telephoning
May I speak to X, please?
Who's calling?
My name is ...
Hold the line please.
Fibak speaking.
Can you give her a message?
Thank you for calling.
The code's 010 42 2, then you dial the number.

Structure—Present simple/present continuous contrast

—Chris is making a phone call to a customer. He makes twenty or thirty calls a day.
—At the moment they are spending very large sums on the health service.
—They usually agree to pay by Letter of Credit.

Unit 3

Structures:	Future **will** and conditional 1
Functional areas:	Persuading Making travel bookings

The story so far: Chris interviewed the Czech journalist, Vaclav Fibak, whose name had been given to him by Laurie Denton. Fibak, in turn, gave him the name of the Purchasing Manager of Medipraha in Prague. Chris then spoke to the foreign branch of Plastech's bank, who were encouraging about the idea of exporting to Czechoslovakia. Finally he arranged to see his Export Manager, Tom Richardson, first thing the next day.

Section A Dialogue and language work

A1 Guided listening

Read these questions before you listen to the story.

1 Tom isn't keen to go to Czechoslovakia. He gives three reasons. What are they?
2 Chris gives four reasons why *he* should go. What are they?
3 What will Chris's itinerary be?

Dialogue

(*There is a knock on the door of Tom Richardson's office.*)

RICHARDSON: Come in, Chris, and sit down. Would you like a cup of coffee?

CHRIS: Yes please, I would ... Thank you.

RICHARDSON: Have you seen that OPEC are going to put another 15% on the price of oil? If it goes on like this, we'll all be bankrupt.

CHRIS: It'll affect our prices, I suppose?

RICHARDSON: Well, it's bound to, eventually. Still, everybody else will be in the same boat, so I expect we'll manage. Now, what can I do for you?

CHRIS: Well, it's about Czechoslovakia. You're going there quite soon, aren't you?

RICHARDSON: Yes, the board decided we should try to get a foot in the door there some time ago, and I've been preparing the ground. I can't say I'm terribly keen.

CHRIS: Why not?

RICHARDSON: Well, for one thing there's an enormous amount to do here, so if I go away it'll be harder for everyone else. Also I'm a bit worried about Eileen. She's still not very strong after the operation.

CHRIS: Oh, I'm sorry to hear that.

RICHARDSON: Oh, she's recovering all right, but you know how it is. Basically, I suppose I'm not very enthusiastic about Comecon business. Even if we do everything right, they may not give us any orders; and if we get a contract, they'll want all sorts of technical information from us. I don't like giving information away, Chris. I never have. But why are you so interested?

CHRIS: Well, to be honest, I'd like you to send me instead.

RICHARDSON: Would you now? Are you after my job, by any chance?

CHRIS: No, of course not, but I think there's a lot to be said for the idea.

RICHARDSON: Oh yes?

CHRIS: Yes. Look, in the first place I'm going to the Vienna conference anyway, so it won't mean a special trip. In the second place, as you said yourself, you're very tied up here at the moment. Then I've managed to get a personal contact, which will help. Last but not least, I'm very keen to go. And I've done my homework, so you needn't worry about that.

RICHARDSON: A personal contact, eh? Who's that?

CHRIS: Well, it's the Medipraha Purchasing Manager, actually. I got his name from a Czech journalist in London. I haven't been in touch with him yet, but it's worth trying, don't you think? I think it would be a good idea to send him a telex today, then if you agree, I'll phone him before I go.

RICHARDSON: *If* you go. You're taking quite a lot for granted, aren't you?

CHRIS: No, not really, Tom. Of course, if you don't like the idea, I'll forget about it. But please think about it. Both Fibak and Druce at the bank are very encouraging about the prospects at the moment.

RICHARDSON: Oh, you've seen Druce as well, have you?

CHRIS: Yes, and he thinks it's a good time for exporters generally, as their Five Year Plan gets under way. And Fibak says they're putting a lot of money into their health service.

RICHARDSON: They get most of their medical equipment from West Germany and the United States, don't they?

CHRIS: Yes, but we can match them for quality, surely? I'd love to have a crack at it, Tom. We've nothing to lose, have we?

RICHARDSON: Well, you make a good case, but I've a feeling I should go myself, as it's a new market.

CHRIS: I can appreciate that. But we're not completely unknown, are we? We've got a good reputation in the DDR and Poland. Surely that's in our favour?

RICHARDSON: I certainly hope so ... All right, Chris, you've persuaded me. I'll clear it with the Managing Director. If we can get your visa fixed, you can go to Prague on the way to Vienna. Sally'll do your bookings. You can see her in a minute. Oh, and by the way, I'd like you to call and see Hofmeier in Frankfurt on the way back. There seems to be a problem ...

(*A few minutes later*)

CHRIS: Sally, can you get this telex off to Prague today, please. I'll confirm that by letter this afternoon. And then can you make my travel arrangements for next week? I'm going to spend a couple of days in Prague before I go to Vienna.

SALLY: Yes, of course. Can you let me have the details?

CHRIS: Yes. First of all I'm going to ...

(*A few minutes later*)

SALLY: Hello? Riverbank Travel? Good morning, this is Plastech Head Office here, Mr Richardson's secretary. I'd like to make some bookings for our Mr Telford, T-E-L-F-O-R-D. He wants to fly from London to Prague on Wednesday the 24th, economy class. Can you also book him a single room in a good hotel near the city centre for the nights of the 24th, 25th and 26th? Have you got that?

Colloquial terms

it's bound to (8) it is certain to; there is no doubt that it will
in the same boat (9) in the same difficult situation
get a foot in the door (13) gain entrance into something
preparing the ground (14) making the first investigations, enquiries and contacts
very tied up (36) very busy with previous engagements
have a crack at it (59) try and do it

A2 Focus on structure—Future **will** and conditional 1

1 Why isn't Tom enthusiastic about Comecon business? What does he say about technical information?
2 What will Chris do
(i) if Tom agrees to let him go to Prague?
(ii) if Tom doesn't agree to let him go to Prague?
3 Tom agrees. What will he do next? What will Sally do?

A3 Focus on function—Persuading

Chris uses several arguments to persuade Tom to let him go to Czechoslovakia. Among them are:

1 his enthusiasm.
2 the quality of Plastech products.
3 Plastech's reputation in other Comecon countries.

What does he actually say?

Focus on function—Making travel bookings

4 How does Sally make
(i) a plane reservation?
(ii) a hotel booking?

A4 Vocabulary

Find phrases from the dialogue to complete these sentences.

1 If a firm, or a person, has no money, they go ______.

2 Are OPEC going to raise their prices? Yes, they're going to ______ ______ ______ ______ ______ ______ ______ ______

3 The situation is the same for everybody. We're all ______ ______ ______ ______.

4 Plastech want to get into a new market. They want a ______ ______ ______ ______ in Czechoslovakia.

5 It's a good idea. There's a lot ______ ______ ______ for it.

6 The idea might work. Anyway, it's ______ ______ don't you think?

7 Our competitors make good products, but so do we. We can ______ ______ ______ ______.

8 Tom must get senior management to agree. He'll ______ ______ with the Managing Director.

9 See Sally. She'll ______ ______ ______.

10 How long is Chris going to be in Prague? He's going to ______ ______ ______ ______ ______ there.

Section B Extension work—Grammar practice

Future tense with **will**

Everyone else will be in the same boat, so I expect we'll manage
It won't mean a special trip ('won't' = 'will not')
I'll confirm that by letter this afternoon

This tense is used to describe future situations and to express intentions. Note that **shall** is an alternative for **will** only after **I** and **we**.

Going to + verb, to express future action, often means the same as **will**. It is, however, used especially to express future intention, or to describe something that is inevitable or very likely indeed.

Conditional 1

If it goes on like this, we'll all be bankrupt
If I go away, it'll be harder for everyone else

In these examples we are imagining possibilities, either in the present or the future. The verb which follows **if** and describes the condition is usually in the present simple. The verb which describes the result is the future with **will**.

I'll phone him before I go
If you go . . .

Note that the present simple is used after 'time' words like **when**, **before**, **after**, **until**, **as soon as**. The future with **will** is used in the main clause.

B1 Fluency practice

Make complete sentences, using the words in brackets.

Example: If Tom ______ (*agree*), Chris ______ (*go*) to Prague.
If Tom agrees, Chris will go to Prague.

1 If we ______ (*get*) an order, they ______ (*want*) all sorts of technical information.
2 If you ______ (*phone*) me tomorrow, I ______ (*give*) you an answer.
3 We ______ (*not get*) a contract if we ______ (*not move*) quickly.
4 If the plane ______ (*be*) on time, we ______ (*arrive*) at two o'clock.
5 If we ______ (*place*) the order today, when ______ we ______ (*receive*) it?
6 Chris ______ (*not go*) to Czechoslovakia if the Managing Director ______ (*not agree*).
7 Tom ______ (*not go*) on overseas trips if his wife ______ (*be*) ill.
8 ______ the letter ______ (*reach*) him in time if we ______ (*send*) it tomorrow?

B2 Free stage

Conditional 1

Tom and Chris are discussing how to send some small orders to various countries. Work in pairs and use the table below to ask and answer questions.

Example: TOM: How long will it take if we send the order to Tokyo by plane?
CHRIS: It'll take 4 days.
TOM: How much will it cost if we send it to Tokyo by plane?
CHRIS: It'll cost $450.

Destination	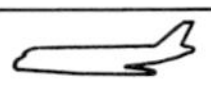		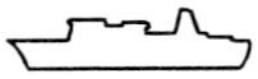		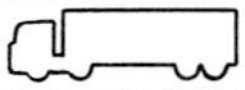	
	Time (days)	Cost ($)	Time (days)	Cost ($)	Time (days)	Cost ($)
Tokyo	4	450	24	210	—	—
Barcelona	3	120	8	84	7	60
Frankfurt	3	90	—	—	7	60
Cairo	5	230	12	150	14	170

Section C Extension work—Functional areas

C1 Persuading

Listen to the extracts from the dialogue. Chris tries to persuade Tom to let him go to Czechoslovakia. Listen to the phrases he uses to persuade him, and then complete the phrases below.

As you said yourself . . .
I've managed to . . .
I'm very keen to . . .
It's worth . . .
I think it would be . . .
Fibak and Druce are . . .
We've nothing . . .

Work in pairs and take the parts of Tom and Chris. At the moment Plastech do not do any business with South America. They have no contacts and there is uncertainty about competition and about the political situation.

Chris should use some of the phrases above, to try to persuade Tom to start an export drive in Bolivia. This is the information Chris has:

(a) very little competition
(b) Bolivia may get grants from World Health Organization
(c) good entry to South American market
(d) his sister is going to marry a Bolivian doctor

Making travel arrangements

Listen again to Sally phoning the travel agent. Work in pairs. One of you is Sally and the other plays the various receptionists and information clerks that Sally speaks to.

	Sally		*Receptionist/clerk*
1	Contact the Ambassador Hotel in Prague to reserve a room for Chris.	1	Confirm the reservation.
2	Contact the Eifelkern Hotel in Frankfurt to reserve a room for Chris.	2	You are full on the 31st.
3	Contact the travel agency and find out about rail travel from Prague to Vienna.	3	Prague–Vienna US$90. Every two hours from 08.00 to 18.00. Seats can be reserved. Collect tickets from tourist office at station.
4	Book a flight from Vienna to Frankfurt on the 31st.	4	Get details of the passenger's requirements and give flight information.

C2 Consolidation

Complete this dialogue. You are talking to your Managing Director. You want to persuade him to send you to the American Trade Fair in Detroit. Practise the dialogue in pairs.

MANAGING DIRECTOR: I'm not sure that we can afford to send you to the American Trade Fair this year.

YOU: ....

MANAGING DIRECTOR: Even if you stay with your cousin, it'll cost about £400 in air fares.

YOU: ....

MANAGING DIRECTOR: I know a lot of potential customers will be there, but I don't think . . .

YOU (*interrupting*): ....

MANAGING DIRECTOR: Yes, it's true business with the States is increasing. Perhaps it is worth keeping in touch with your contacts there. All right, then, I agree.

YOU: ....

MANAGING DIRECTOR: Yes. Ask her to come and see me when she's finished making the arrangements with the travel agent.

Section D Listening work

D1 Structure exercise—Conditional 1

Tom Richardson and Chris are discussing next year's sales prospects for some of their products. You are Tom. Look at the table below, and ask Chris for the details you need to complete it. Use the prompts to help you ask the questions, and fill in the answers as you hear them.

Example: FC 24s/give bigger discounts?

TOM: *How many FC24s will we sell if we give bigger discounts?*

CHRIS: We'll sell about 25,000.

TOM: *And if we don't give bigger discounts?*

CHRIS: We'll sell about 10,000.

1 FC 24s/give bigger discounts?
2 FC 30s/increase our advertising?
3 CT 20s/keep our delivery dates?
4 CT 15s/improve our servicing?
5 CT 100s/raise the price?

Product	Sales forecasts	
FC 24	25000	
FC 30		
CT 20		
CT 15		
CT 100		

D2 Story extract—Focus on function

Listen to the extract from the dialogue, then listen and repeat.

D3 Listening for information

Chris is giving Sally instructions for his travel arrangements. Listen to their conversation and fill in the table below.

Chris Telford—Itinerary for Sales Promotion visit

Destination	Departure date	Duration of visit	Hotel	Reason for visit	Other arrangements
PRAGUE					

Use the information in Chris's itinerary to answer the questions you will hear. You are Chris.

Example: How long are you going to stay in Prague, Chris?
I'm going to stay for three nights.

Section E Group work

Planning a journey

In this activity, one student takes the part of a travel agent, who has details of travel services and schedules. Other students work in pairs, as businessmen. They must obtain travel information from the travel agent, make plans for their journey and then make bookings with the travel agent.

Instructions to the travel agent

1 Check the availability of all the facilities requested and inform your customers.
2 Fill in a Travel Confirmation slip, like the one below, for each pair of businessmen.

From	To	Method of travel	Date	Departure time	Confirmed
Hotel booking Hotel [ ]		From [ ]		To [ ]	

Turn to pages 95 and 96 in the group work information section at the back of the book, where you will find the necessary travel details.

Instructions to the businessmen

1 You are a pair of businessmen, A and B, who work in London and have to go to Copenhagen together on business. Decide which of you is A and which is B.
2 Today is Monday 12th. It is 12 noon. You can leave London at any time.
3 You must arrive in Copenhagen by 5pm on Wednesday 14th, and you must be back in London by 2pm on Saturday 17th.
4 You should consider these factors:
(a) completing your programme of visits and maintaining your schedule
(b) economy (your company is trying to minimize unnecessary expenditure)
(c) personal preference (try to persuade your colleague to follow your suggestions)

5 You must spend at least one hour (preferably more) with each of the following in Copenhagen:
(a) Larsen AB
(b) Moller & Co
(c) Danske Veritas (closed on Thursday)
(d) Odense Shipping
(e) Ove Jensen & Co
(f) Commercial Attaché, British Embassy (not available after 12 noon, Friday)

6 If you can fit in a visit to Baake Kunststoffwerke, Hamburg, you will each receive a substantial bonus—but from the Company's point of view the visit is not necessary at this time.

7 Your individual preferences are:

A

You do not like travelling by air because you get airsick.

You want to go to an important lunch engagement on Tuesday 13th from 12.00 to 14.30.

You want to spend as little money as possible in line with the Company's economy drive.

B

You get very seasick.

You want to go to Hamburg very much.

You are not worried about expense as long as you do the necessary business.

Reminder of key points in Unit 3

Functional areas

Persuading
There's a lot to be said for it.
I'm very keen to ...
I'd like you to ...
It's worth trying ...
I think it would be a good idea to ...
If you agree, I'll ...
Please think about it.
Surely ...

Making travel bookings
I'd like to make some bookings.
He wants to fly from X to Y on Monday.
Can you book a good hotel near ...?
I'm going to spend a couple of days in ...
You can go to Prague on the way to Vienna.

Structure: Future **will** and conditional 1

—I'll clear it with the Managing Director.
—It won't mean a special trip.
—If it goes on like this, we'll all be bankrupt.

Unit 4

Structure:	Past simple/past continuous contrast
Functional areas:	Asking for information Giving directions

The story so far: Chris has persuaded his Export Manager, Tom Richardson, to send him to Prague to try to get some business with Medipraha, the Czech Government Agency for the Health Service. He has sent a telex to Mr Novotny, the Medipraha Purchasing Manager, and he then writes to confirm his visit. On Wednesday 24th he goes to Heathrow airport.

Section A Dialogue and language work

A1 Guided listening

Read these questions before you listen to the story.

1 Chris wants to get two things before take-off. What are they?
2 He has a surprise on the plane. What is it?
3 Why is Ingrid going to Prague?
4 Why does the hotel recommend Tuzex as a good place to shop?

Dialogue

CHRIS: Can you tell me where the Czech Airlines counter is, please?
OFFICIAL: Yes, certainly, sir. Go through those doors and turn right. You'll see a row of check-in counters on the far side of the hall, past the Thomas Cook office. CSA is the fourth one along, next to Singapore Airlines.
CHRIS: Thank you very much.
CSA: Good morning. Ticket please. May I see your passport, sir? ... Thank you Mr Telford, here you are. Your flight will be called in about twenty minutes.
CHRIS: Thank you. I say, could you possibly tell me how much alcohol I can take into Czechoslovakia, please?
CSA: One litre of spirits, or two litres of wine.
CHRIS: And can I buy duty-free spirits on board the plane?
CSA: Yes, certainly. But there's a much better selection in the duty-free shop here. That's on the first floor, near the restaurant.
CHRIS: Yes, I think I'll go up there. Oh, and by the way, do you know of a good Czech phrase book?
CSA: Please take a copy of this leaflet of ours. It has some useful phrases.
CHRIS: Thank you.

(*In the duty-free shop*)

CHRIS: I'll take these, please.

LOUDSPEAKER: Attention please. Czech Airlines announce the departure . . .

SHOP ASSISTANT: Thank you, sir. That's £8.65. Will that be all?

LOUDSPEAKER: Flight CS416 to Prague. Will passengers . . .

CHRIS: Yes thanks. Can I pay by credit card?

LOUDSPEAKER: . . . please proceed to Gate * * * for boarding.

CHRIS: What was that? What did she say? Gate what?

SHOP ASSISTANT: Sorry, sir, I wasn't listening.

CHRIS: Excuse me, what gate number is it for the flight to Prague, please?

CSA: Gate 21, sir.

CHRIS: Thank you very much.

(*On the plane*)

CHRIS: Is this Row C, please? Good Heavens, Ingrid, it's you!

INGRID: Hello, Chris. I thought I saw you earlier, while I was changing some money, but then you disappeared. What happened?

CHRIS: Well, I didn't come through with the rest. As a matter of fact I was just buying some whisky when they called the flight, and I nearly missed the plane. Now tell me, how is it that you're going to Prague, if you don't mind me asking?

INGRID: I'm going to see my relations.

CHRIS: In Prague? But you're English, surely?

INGRID: Well, I'm half English. My mother was Czech.

CHRIS: Was?

INGRID: Oh, she died when I was little, but I still go to see the family, when I can.

(*The plane takes off*)

The last time I went was in December two years ago, and it snowed all the time I was there. I've never been so cold in my life. But why are you going there, may I ask?

CHRIS: Oh, I'm going to see the purchasing people in their health service. I say, if by any chance you're free one evening, perhaps we could ...

(*They arrive at Prague airport.*)

IMMIGRATION OFFICER: Passport, please. Thank you. How long will you be in Czechoslovakia, Mr Telford?

CHRIS: For three nights.

IMMIGRATION OFFICER: And what is the purpose of your visit?

CHRIS: I'm on business. I'm here to visit Medipraha, your health service agency.

IMMIGRATION OFFICER: I see. Will you go on to Customs, please? Along this corridor and through the door at the end ...

(*Later, at the hotel*)

RECEPTIONIST: Welcome to the Hotel Ambassador, Mr Telford. Your room number is 404. May I have your passport please? Oh, and here is a message for you from Medipraha. They will contact you here in the morning.

CHRIS: Thank you. Oh, by the way, can you suggest somewhere near the hotel where I can buy souvenirs?

RECEPTIONIST: Yes, you should go to the Tuzex Stores, the Government stores that sell things for export. You can buy direct with foreign currency, and the prices are very reasonable. They stay open quite late. There's one near here.

CHRIS: Thanks. Can you tell me how to get there?

RECEPTIONIST: Yes. It's quite easy. You turn right out of the hotel, go across the big square, go straight up the Stanislavski Prospekt for about two hundred metres, and turn left ...

A2 Focus on structure—Past simple/past continuous contrast

1 Did Ingrid see Chris at the airport before they got on the plane?
2 Did she speak to him? Why not?
3 What was she doing when she saw Chris?
4 Where was he when they called the flight? What was he doing?

A3 Focus on function—Asking for information

Chris asks for information about

1 the duty-free allowance.
2 help in learning the Czech language.
3 the gate number.

What exactly does he say?

Focus on function—Giving directions

Chris needs to know the way to

4 the Customs Office.
5 the Tuzex Stores.

What directions is he given?

A4

Vocabulary

Use the story to complete these sentences.

1 CSA is the fourth check-in ______ in the hall.
2 At the airport, what will happen in about 20 minutes? Chris's flight ______ ______ ______.
3 You get more choice in the shop. There's a ______ ______ ______.
4 Chris doesn't need a dictionary, but he does want a ______ ______.
5 He wants to learn a few ______ ______ of Czech.
6 He doesn't pay cash for the whisky, he pays ______ ______ ______.
7 Ingrid is going to Prague to ______ ______ ______.
8 The customs office is ______ ______ ______ and through the door.
9 When Chris arrives at the hotel there is a ______ for him.
10 Prices at Tuzex aren't expensive. They're ______ ______.

Section B Extension work—Grammar practice

Past simple/past continuous contrast

What did he say? Sorry, sir, I wasn't listening
I saw you earlier while I was changing some money, but then you disappeared. What happened?
I was just buying some whisky when they called the flight

The most usual use of the past continuous tense is to describe the background to another event in the past. The event itself is described in the past simple.

These two tenses are often used in one sentence with words like **when, while**: **The telephone rang when I was having my dinner**. The past simple describes something that happened in the middle of another action in the past, which is described by the past continuous. If one action is a direct result of the other, they are both described by the past simple: **When the telephone rang, I answered it** (immediately afterwards).

B1

Fluency practice

Make complete sentences with the verbs in brackets. Note that in some of the sentences below more than one answer is possible. Where two answers are possible, the meaning sometimes changes.

Example: We ______ (*buy*) some duty-free Scotch while we ______ (*wait*) in the lounge.
We bought some duty-free Scotch while we were waiting in the lounge.

1 The Customs officials ______ (*check*) my luggage when they ______ (*see*) the extra cigarettes.
2 Chris ______ (*drink*) a lot of whisky when he ______ (*stay*) in Scotland.
3 He ______ (*not know*) Ingrid ______ (*go*) to Prague before Vienna.

4 I ______ (*work*) last night so I ______ (*not see*) the film.
5 How long ______ you (*wait*) before the plane ______ (*take off*)?
6 What ______ Chris ______ (*do*) when Ingrid ______ (*see*) him?
7 The Chairman ______ (*sign*) the contract when he ______ (*hear*) the good news.
8 We ______ (*go*) to write to you last week but we ______ (*be*) very busy.
9 We ______ (*finish*) dinner and then we ______ (*go*) to a night club.
10 She ______ (*tell*) me about the new product while we ______ (*have*) lunch.

B2

Free stage

Look at the pictures below. Work in pairs and ask and answer two questions about each picture.

Example: Picture 1

(a) Past continuous
What were they doing when the bus arrived?
They were talking or *They were standing in the queue.*

(b) Past simple
What did they do when the bus arrived?
They got on it.

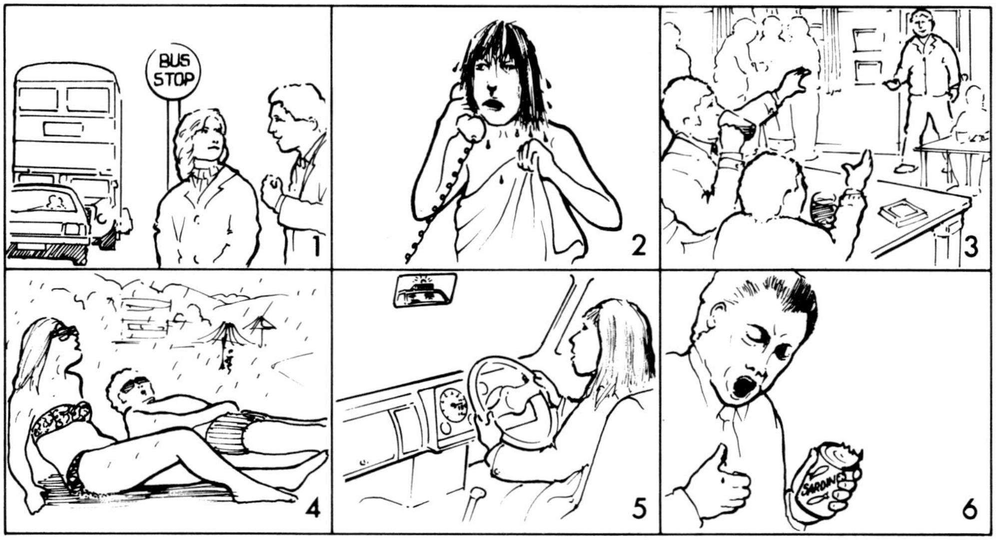

Section C Extension work—Functional areas

C1

Asking for information

Listen again to Chris's conversation at the Czech Airlines check-in desk. Work in pairs, and construct a dialogue based on the notes on page 34. Then practise the dialogue, taking it in turns to be the traveller.

Traveller

You have just arrived in Bangkok. Find out
(a) the latest exchange rate
(b) where you can get a haircut
(c) where you can see some Thai dancing

Receptionist

Try to help the traveller.

Now listen to the questions the Immigration Officer asks when Chris arrives in Prague. Work in pairs again.

Traveller

You need a visa to the Central Asian Republic very quickly. Ask at the Embassy.

Embassy official

Find out why the traveller wants a visa, and any other details you need.

Giving directions

Listen again to the directions from the hotel to the Tuzex store. Then work in pairs, and, using the map and the notes below, practise giving directions.

Traveller 1

You are at the castle. Ask for directions to the Tuzex store [T].

Prague resident

Try to help the traveller.

Traveller 2

You are at the Tuzex store. Ask for directions to your hotel [H].

Prague resident

Try to help the traveller.

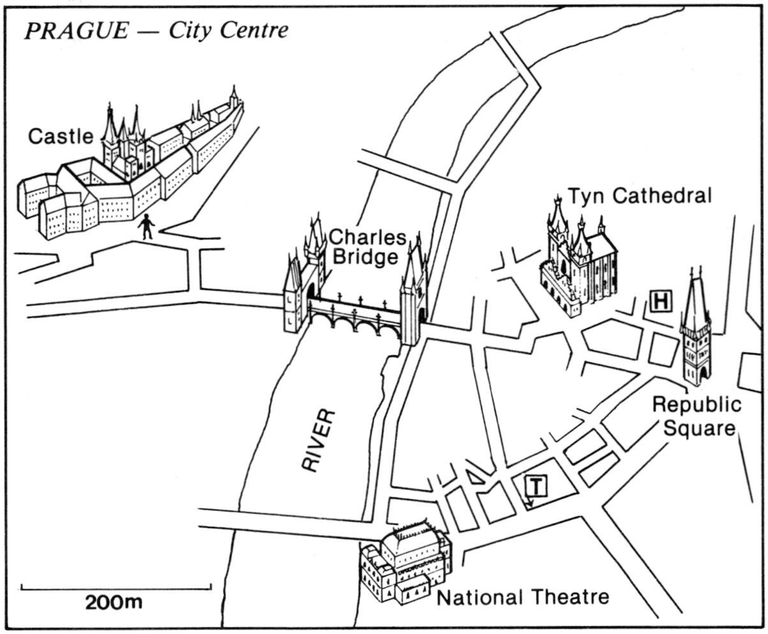

C2 Consolidation

Complete the conversation at the local Tourist Information Office. Then practise it with a partner.

YOU: ....

OFFICIAL: The coaches leave every two hours and do a round trip of the city.

YOU: ....

OFFICIAL: About 90 minutes.

YOU: ....

OFFICIAL: From the bus station in the city centre. The next one will go in about 25 minutes.

YOU: ....

OFFICIAL: Go straight along this road and it's on the left. You'll see it easily.

YOU: ....

OFFICIAL: There should be plenty of opportunity to take photos. The coaches stop near all the main places of interest.

Section D Listening work

D1 Structure exercise—Past simple/past continuous contrast

Look at the pictures and listen to the tape. Now look at the pictures again and talk to the President of your company on the telephone.

D2 Story extract—Focus on function

Listen to the extract from the dialogue. Then listen and repeat.

D3 Listening for information

Listen to Sally describing a day trip from England to France. Make notes about:

(a) the number of people who went
(b) the method of travel (there and back)
(c) how they spent the morning
(d) where they had lunch
(e) the afternoon programme
(f) the weather

You will now hear some questions. Use your notes to help you answer them.

Section E Group work

Talking about travel

Stage 1: Each of you will take one or two minutes to tell the class what you bought on your last trip to another country—and why
(a) for youself
(b) for a close relative, as a present.

Stage 2: Form groups of three or four people. Each group, after an initial discussion, makes a list of five recommended souvenirs from the region you are now in, in order of preference. No souvenir must cost more than £30 (or equivalent).

You should then suggest the best place to buy the items you have chosen, and be prepared to give directions on how to get there.

Reminder of key points in Unit 4

Functional areas

Asking for information
Can you tell me?
Could you possibly tell me . . .?
Do you know . . .?
Can I . . .?
Excuse me, what . . .?
How long . . .?
Can you suggest somewhere . . .?

Giving directions
Go through those doors and turn right.
It's the fourth one along.
It's on the first floor.
Go across the square.
Go straight on.

Structure—Past simple/past continuous contrast

—I was buying some whisky when they called the flight.
—I wasn't listening (when they made the announcement).
—I nearly missed the plane.

Unit 5

Structure:	Passive
Functional areas:	Describing production Requesting and giving specifications

The story so far: To his surprise Chris met Ingrid on the plane to Prague. He suggested they met one evening during their stay, and checked in at his hotel. He received a message from Medipraha saying they would contact him the following day.

Section A Dialogue and language work

A1 Guided listening

Read these questions before you listen to the story.

1 Why did Mr Tyborski come to the hotel?
2 What kind of hospital do they visit?
3 Why is Chris interested in the boxes in the operating theatre?
4 What does Dr Krusina ask Chris about?
5 What does Chris explain to Mr Tyborski?

Dialogue

(*At the hotel reception*)

TYBORSKI: Mr Telford? My name is Tyborski, from Medipraha.

CHRIS: How do you do?

TYBORSKI: I've been asked to look after you. Mr Novotny was called to a meeting this morning. You'll see him later this afternoon. Now, my car is parked outside. We have a fairly short drive to one of our new hospitals, in the suburb of Praha-Dejvice. The building was finished three months ago. The services have been installed—electricity, gas, water and so on, and now it's being decorated and equipped. We hope everything will be done by the end of August.

CHRIS: Is it a general hospital, or does it specialize in certain areas?

TYBORSKI: Oh, general, almost everything will be treated there, but there *will* be an especially large paediatric department, for children you know, and later on a research unit will be set up for skin diseases, and other nervous diseases like asthma. It should be . . .

CHRIS (*interrupting*): Did you say asthma? My father has asthma, and he says it's caused by the weather.

TYBORSKI (*laughing*): Yes, I think I agree. I sometimes suffer badly myself, when it's dusty and dry.

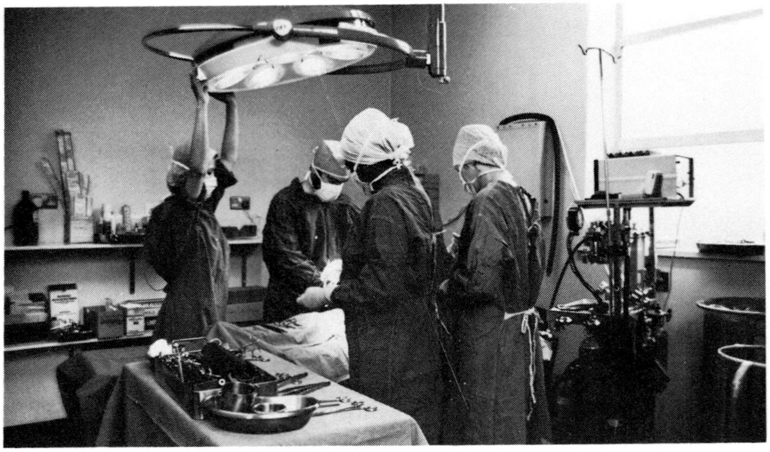

In the operating theatre

(*At the hospital*)

TYBORSKI: Mr Telford, this is Dr Krusina. He will be in charge of the surgical and post-operative facilities.

CHRIS: How do you do, Dr Krusina?

KRUSINA: How do you do, Mr Telford? First of all, I'm going to show you our new operating theatre. It's very modern.

CHRIS: It looks very impressive. I see you buy from the United States.

KRUSINA: Pardon?

CHRIS: These boxes, they're from the United States, aren't they? I know the name Patrician, it's the trademark of PRH Universal, in Chicago, isn't it?

KRUSINA: I believe so, yes.

CHRIS: Yes, they're big competitors of ours. I'm sure we can match them for quality, and I'm quite certain we can beat them for delivery.

KRUSINA: Please, Mr Telford, I'm only a doctor, not a buyer—but I am interested in the range and quality of your equipment. Can you supply anaesthetic and intensive care systems?

CHRIS: Certainly, and in a wide range of sizes.

KRUSINA: What exactly is the internal diameter of the endotracheal tubes?

CHRIS: They go from 2mm to 11mm.

KRUSINA: Aha, and how long are they?

CHRIS: They're supplied in standard 20cm lengths.

KRUSINA: I see. And they're made of PVC, I suppose.

CHRIS: Yes, they're available in transparent or in translucent PVC.

KRUSINA: How long is the guarantee?

CHRIS: Five years minimum on all products. Seven years for the Blue Streak range.

KRUSINA: Does that guarantee apply to infant care systems as well?

CHRIS: Yes, that applies to all our products.

KRUSINA: Then I'm sure Mr Tyborski and his colleagues will be interested in what you have to offer.

TYBORSKI: Yes, indeed ... Mr Telford, I'm very interested in the manufacturing process. Could you tell me how these catheters are made?

CHRIS: With pleasure. The basic raw materials for our products are PVC powder and plasticizer —incidentally a lot of this is imported from Romania. The powder and plasticizer are mixed together in about one hundred and fifty different recipes, depending on the purpose. The tubing is extruded from the PVC pellets and then it is cooled in a tank of water and cut into lengths. At this stage....

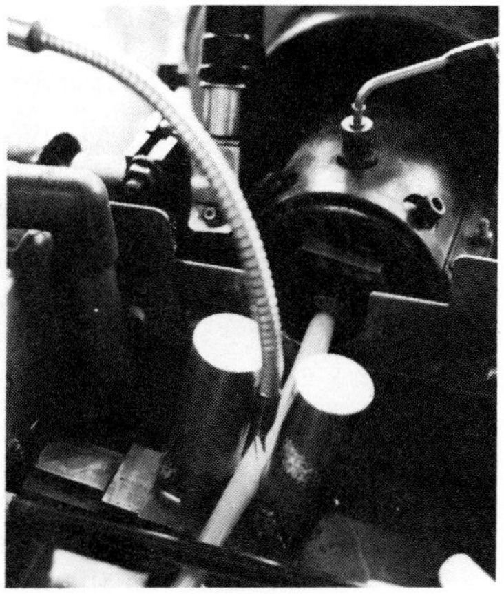

Extrusion of medical grade PVC tubing

Then after assembly the products are packed into blister packs and carefully sterilized. That's very important, as you can imagine.

TYBORSKI: Yes indeed, Mr Telford. It's all very interesting. Now, have you any questions before we move on?

CHRIS: Well, I was just wondering if Dr Krusina could tell me how many beds ...

A2

Focus on structure—Passive

Listen again to Mr Tyborski's description of the new hospital on the tape.

1 What happened three months ago?
2 What does he say about electricity, gas and water?
3 What is happening there now?
4 What does he say about 'the end of August'?

A3

Focus on function—Describing processes

The passive is often used for describing processes.
Listen to Chris's description of the production methods. What happens to:

1 the PVC powder and the plasticizer?
2 the tubing after it has been cooled?
3 the various components after assembly?

Focus on function—Requesting and giving specifications

Dr Krusina wants information about

4 the types of product.
5 the size of tubes.
6 the guarantee.

What questions does he ask?

Chris tells him about

7 the sizes.
8 the lengths.
9 the material.

What exactly does he say?

A4

Vocabulary

Use the story to complete these sentences.

1 Mr Novotny couldn't meet Chris because he ______ ______ to a meeting.
2 Mr Tyborski's car is ______ ______ the hotel.
3 Praha-Dejvice is a ______ ______ Prague.
4 A research unit will be ______ ______ in the hospital.
5 Dr Krusina has a lot of responsibility, because he will be ______ ______ ______ a hospital department.
6 ______ operate in the operating theatre.
7 Patrician is the ______ of PRH Universal.
8 A minimum 5-year guarantee ______ to all Plastech products.
9 PVC powder and plasticizer are the basic ______ ______ of the products.
10 The various parts of a product, which are put together during assembly, are its ______.

Section B

Extension work—Grammar practice

Passive

Mr Novotny was called to a meeting this morning
Asthma is caused by the weather

The passive here emphasizes 'Mr Novotny' and 'asthma' because they are mentioned first. That is, they are the most important things we are thinking about. 'The weather causes asthma' means nearly the same as the example; but it suggests we are more interested in the weather than in the disease.

The building was finished three months ago and the services have been installed
Everything will be treated there. Later a research unit will be set up

These impersonal statements tell us what happens, but not who does it. Sometimes we do not know. Generally the persons responsible are not mentioned because they are not considered to be important. This use is frequent both in reporting and in scientific English.

How are catheters made?

This example demonstrates all the points mentioned above.

B1

Fluency practice

Complete the sentences below, using a passive form of the verb in brackets.

Example: The building ______ (*finish*) three months ago.
The building was finished three months ago.

Past simple

1 The cathedral ______ (*build*) in 1436.
2 Chris ______ (*impress*) by the old town of Prague.
3 These boxes ______ (*deliver*) yesterday. They ______ (*send*) from the USA.

Present simple

4 Each item ______ (*check*) ten times during manufacture.
5 This product ______ (*guarantee*) for five years.
6 The tubes ______ (*make*) of PVC. They ______ (*produce*) in sizes from 2mm to 11mm.

Present continuous

7 The hospital ______ (*decorate*) at the moment.
8 A lot of new equipment ______ (*install*) this week.
9 No operations ______ (*carry out*) at present.

Present perfect

10 The equipment from PRH just ______ (*deliver*).
11 Chris ______ (*show*) the new facilities, and is now talking to Mr Tyborski.
12 ______ the operating theatre ______ (*equip*) yet?

Future

13 A research unit ______ (*set up*) next year.
14 In future, skin diseases ______ (*treat*) there.
15 Chris ______ (*ask*) a lot more questions before he can make a sale.

B2

Free stage

We saw in exercise A3 how the passive is used to describe a process. Put the nine pictures below in the right sequence to illustrate how a cotton shirt is made, and how it reaches the distributor. Work in pairs. Describe the process. Use these verbs to help you (they are not in the correct order):

to take   to send   to pick   to make up   to weave (weave:wove:woven)   to grow   to inspect   to pack

You will also find this vocabulary useful in your description:

material   textile mill   plantation   warehouse   cotton mill   polythene bags

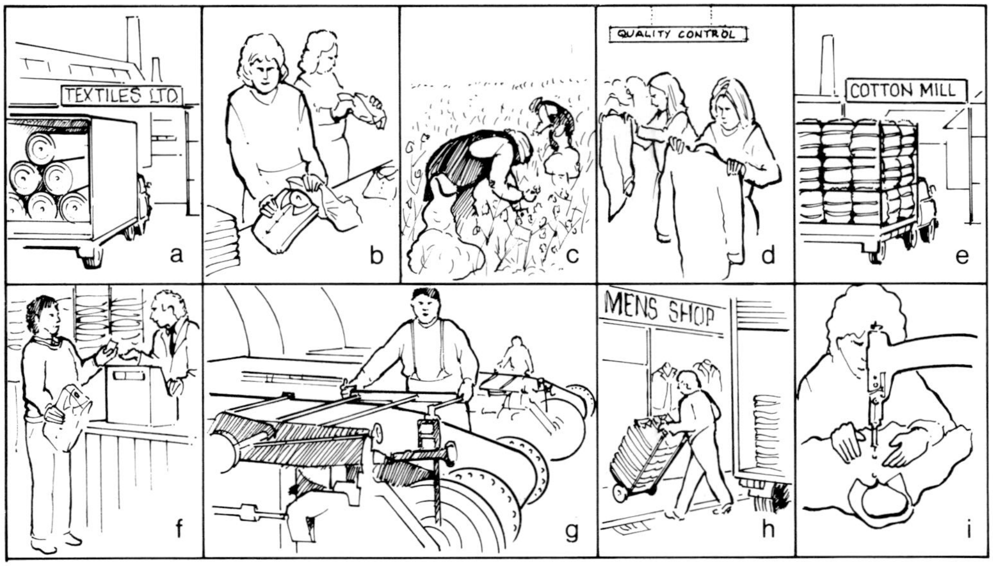

Section C Extension work—Functional areas

C1

Describing production

Look through Chris's description of the production process for medical tubes again. Now work out your own description of the stages these articles go through, from raw materials to consumer.

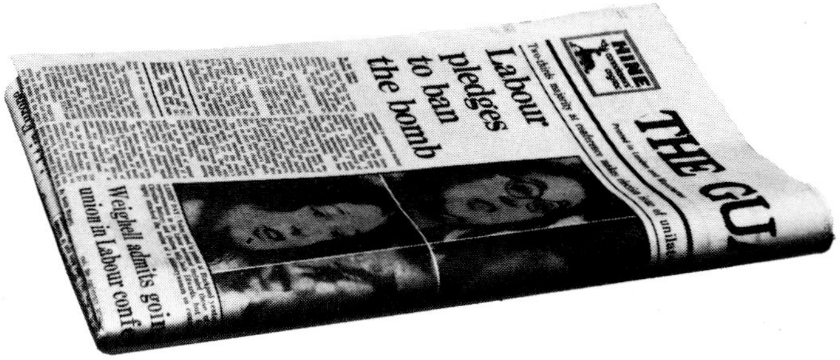

Requesting and giving specifications

Work in pairs. One student is selling portable cassette players like the one illustrated; the other is a customer who needs information.

Customer

Ask questions to find out about:

- the size
- the weight
- the price
- the power output
- the guarantee
- the power source
- the number of controls
- accessories

Salesman

Use this catalogue information to answer the customer's questions:

SUPER STEREO FOR UNDER £30

At only 280 grammes this cassette player is one of the lightest on the market. It comes complete with stereo headphones, and other accessories include a holster and a strap for ease of carrying. It fits comfortably into your pocket as it measures only 29.5 x 140 x 80 mm. It operates on two internal AM3/HP7 batteries, or two HP2 batteries in an external auxiliary pack which give over 60 hours of playback time. The main controls (FORWARD, STOP, FAST FORWARD and REWIND) are touch sensitive, and each machine carries a one year guarantee. Unbeatable value at only £29.99.

C2 Consolidation

You are asking a friend for the specifications of a common object, and trying to guess what it is. Complete the conversation and practise it with a partner.

YOU: ....

FRIEND: Mainly glass, but there's a small metal fitting.

YOU: ....

FRIEND: The diameter ranges from very small to quite large.

YOU: ....

FRIEND: Well, I suppose the average household one has a diameter of about 8cm.

YOU: ....

FRIEND: No. It's pear-shaped, and hollow.

YOU: ....

FRIEND: Just a few grammes.

YOU: ....

FRIEND: Oh yes, very common and very useful, but only at certain times of the day. Some people prefer another type, which is long and cylindrical. Can you guess what it is?

YOU: ....

Section D Listening work

D1 Structure exercise—Passive

Look at the completion schedule for the new hospital. Using this information, answer the questions you will hear on the tape.

Examples: Have the services been completed in the children's ward?
Yes, they have.

Has the children's ward been decorated yet?
No, it's being decorated at the moment.

Has the equipment for the children's ward been ordered?
Yes, it was ordered two months ago.

Has it been installed?
No. It'll be installed next week.

Hospital completion schedule—Progress report

Ward	Services completed	Decoration	Equipment - when ordered	Equipment - installation
Children's Ward	✓	at the moment	two months ago	next week
Men's Surgical Ward	✓	last week	last April	at the moment
Women's Surgical Ward	next week	not yet	at the moment	by the end of the year

D2

Story extract—Focus on function

Listen to the extract from the dialogue. Then listen and repeat.

D3

Listening for information

You are going to hear Chris giving Mr Tyborski the full details of the production process for catheters. Before you listen, study the words below.

Controlled environment assembly unit – or 'clean air' room

catheter	blow moulding
extruded	calibrated
PVC pellets	blister pack
radio-opaque	sterilized

As you listen make notes about:
(a) the raw materials—what are they? where are they imported from? what happens to them?
(b) tubing—how is it made? what happens to it?
(c) 'half ready' products—what is done?
(d) blue line—why?
(e) attachments—how and where are they made?
(f) 'clean air' room—what happens?
(g) packing—how?
(h) before distribution—what happens?

Now use your notes to answer the questions you will hear.

Section E Group work

'How does the system work?'

Form two groups, Group A and Group B. Each group will read a text. Group A will study the text about Access cards (on page 45), and Group B will study the text about AA Vehicle Security (on pages 97 and 98 in the group work information section).
Discuss any difficult words, or anything you do not understand, with the other students in your group. You will need a dictionary. Then decide which are the most important points in your text, and take notes on them. Make sure that everyone in the group knows as much as possible about how the system works. The teacher may ask you first to study the text for homework.

Now close your books and do not look at them again. Form pairs, with one person from each group. You must try to learn as much as possible about the system your partner has studied, and tell him everything you have learned about the system you have studied.

Re-join your group and put together all the information you have got from members of the other group. The teacher will now ask you questions to find out how much information you have exchanged.

Why should I have an Access card?

Q Why should I have an Access card?
A It makes shopping a lot simpler (especially these days when a single note doesn't go very far). And you won't have to worry whether you're carrying enough cash.
You'll be welcomed wherever you go. After a short time with your NatWest Access card, you'll wonder how you ever managed without one.

Q Where can I use an Access card?
A Next time you're in the High Street, look at how many good shops, garages, hotels and restaurants display an Access sign. And remember, it's like this in every High Street in the country. Put another way, if you are buying furniture or a television, dining out, travelling or just buying clothes, simply use your Access card.

Q Can I use it abroad?
A Of course! Just use your Access card as you do in this country.

Q How much will it cost me to get a card?
A Nothing. Not even the price of a stamp. The attached application form is pre-paid.

Q How much can I spend with an Access card?
A As much as you wish up to the agreed credit limit on your NatWest Access account. We will advise you from time to time what your credit limit is.

Q What do you mean by 'credit limit'?
A A credit limit is the maximum sum of money that can be owed to Access at any one time. You are advised of your credit limit when you receive your card or when there is a change made to it by us – it is up to you how much and how often you use it.

Q Can I get cash with my Access card?
A Yes – subject to the amount available within your credit limit. There are 10,000 bank branches in the U.K displaying the Access sign where you can get a cash advance, and when travelling abroad you may draw up to £100 a day in the local currency from most banks displaying the Access, MasterCard or Eurocard signs.

Q How do I know how much I have spent?
A We send you a clear and detailed statement every month. This shows the total amount you owe us and your credit limit.

Q How much do I have to repay each month?
A This is where an Access card really scores. Because you can choose how much you repay each month. Pay as little as £5 or 5% of the total balance outstanding whichever is the greater. Or more if you wish and you have 25 days from the date of your statement for your repayment to reach Access.

Q Does this mean that I can spread repayments over several months?
A Yes. This is one of the real benefits of having an Access card. All you do is make the minimum payment each month. The remaining balance is carried forward and attracts interest at 2.25% per month: this rate of interest may be varied at the Bank's discretion.

Q How do I renew my Access card?
A You don't need to do anything. We will send you a new card before your old one runs out. However, either side can choose to close the account at any time.

Q What if I already have a cheque card?
A You will still find an Access card useful – particularly for all those purchases over £50. Additionally you can take extended credit on your NatWest Access account to cover expensive items.

Q What happens if I lose my Access card?
A Telephone us immediately and confirm in writing within 7 days; your responsibility then ceases. The maximum liability is £25, but it would not be our intention to make any claim against you should the card be misused through no fault of your own.

Q Can I arrange for someone else to use my Access account?
A Yes, by applying for an additional card on your account. This card can be in the name of any one person who must be at least 18 years of age. Just complete the section on the application form.

Q How much interest do I pay?
A If you settle for your purchases in full each month within 25 days of the statement date then you pay no interest at all.
The annual percentage rate of charge is 30.6%. This is based on the maximum annual rate of interest arrived at without making allowance for the time between buying the goods and the date of your statement. In practice, apart from cash advances, the annual rate of interest will vary downwards depending on the period of borrowing.

Q So how do I apply for a card?
A If you are at least 18 years of age just fill in the attached form and post it today.

The Conditions of Use, including the rate of interest, may be varied at the Bank's discretion at any time.

Reminder of key points in Unit 5

Functional areas

Describing production
The raw materials are ...
A lot of this is imported from ...
'half-ready' products
The attachments are made ...
It's a new method.
All the components are calibrated.
After assembly they're packed in ...

Requesting and giving specifications
What exactly is the internal diameter?
They go from 2mm to 11mm.
They're supplied in standard lengths.
They're available in transparent PVC.
How long is the guarantee?

Structure: Passive

—It's being decorated.
—It was finished three months ago.
—Everything will be done by the end of August.
—It is caused by the weather.
—The services have been installed.

Unit 6

Structure:	Comparatives and superlatives
Functional areas:	Comparing quality and performance Explaining processes

The story so far: Chris has met Mr Tyborski, from Medipraha, and has visited one of the State's new hospitals in a suburb of Prague. Here he saw that some of the new equipment was supplied by an American company competing with Plastech. He told Tyborski and a senior doctor at the hospital about Plastech's products, and described the production processes to them.

Section A Dialogue and language work

A1 Guided listening

Read these questions before you listen to the story.

1 What is the first subject that Mr Novotny and Chris discuss?
2 What sort of medical equipment is Mr Novotny particularly interested in?
3 Who is the American in the Ambassador bar?
4 What do you think Ingrid and Chris had for dinner?

Dialogue

(*In Mr Novotny's office*)

NOVOTNY: Ah, Mr Telford, come in. It's nice to see you.

CHRIS: How do you do, Mr Novotny. Thank you for looking after me so well.

NOVOTNY: Not at all. Now, you have been out to Praha-Dejvice, I believe. How did you find it?

CHRIS: Very impressive. Is it the biggest of your new hospitals?

NOVOTNY: No, there's one in another suburb which is the same size. There are two in provincial capitals which are much bigger. The other two in Prague aren't so large, but they're all better equipped than our older hospitals. We're very proud of them.

CHRIS: I'm sure you are. Just as we, in my company, are proud of the equipment we produce.

NOVOTNY: I hope you'll tell me all about it, Mr Telford; but of course you realize that through our contacts elsewhere we already know quite a lot about both your company and your products ...

CHRIS: ... so you see, our Chief Chemist tests the materials for the necessary qualities and as he works closely with the designers of the products, it's possible to ...

NOVOTNY (*interrupting*): Excuse me, but what are these 'necessary qualities'?

CHRIS: It depends. Most of our products are made from PVC, but they differ in many ways. Some must be stronger than others, some must be very flexible. Tubes which go inside the body must have the smoothest possible surface. I believe we have a wider range than most other companies, and everything is sterilized by a process that's second to none. I can assure you that these tubes ...

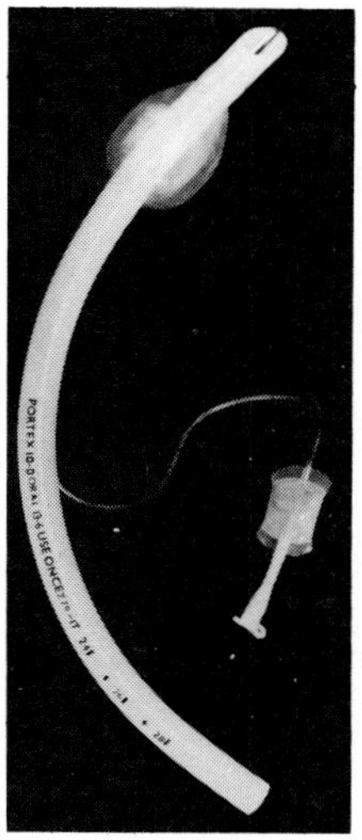

PVC products for use in hospitals

NOVOTNY (*interrupting*): Very good, Mr Telford. Now, I'd like to hear about something that's more sophisticated than these tubes and pipes. What about equipment for open-heart surgery?

CHRIS: Well, of course that's the most difficult field of all. The heart is disconnected while the surgeon repairs it. This means that the blood must be pumped through a machine which does the same job as the heart and lungs. Naturally all connections between this heart-lung machine and the body must be of the best possible quality. We believe ours are smoother and stronger than anyone else's. We make these open-heart sets to the specific requirements of each hospital, and I must stress again that our company's quality control is first-rate.

NOVOTNY: Fine. Well, that's all very interesting. Now I must have a talk with my colleagues. Can we meet again tomorrow morning? ...

(*That evening, Ingrid comes to the Ambassador to meet Chris for dinner.*)

INGRID: A bourbon and water, please.

BARMAN: Certainly, madam.

AMERICAN VOICE: Say, I see you drink American. Will you have a drink with me?

INGRID: That's very kind, but my date will be here in a minute. Are you alone here?

AMERICAN: I am tonight. My pals have gone on to Poland.

INGRID: Are you on holiday?

AMERICAN: Hell, no, we've been selling them equipment for all their hospitals. I'm with PRH, in Chicago, Illinois. We've not clinched any deals yet, but I reckon we've got it about sewn up.

INGRID: Is there no competition in your line of business?

AMERICAN: The Germans are pretty good, but there's no one else that bothers us.

INGRID: I see.

CHRIS (*arriving*): Ingrid. I'm sorry to keep you waiting.

AMERICAN: This your date? Hi there! Have a nice time ...

(*The American leaves.*)

CHRIS: Who's that?

INGRID: I'll tell you about him. But first, where shall we eat? There's a restaurant called the Pelikan near here. It does local specialities, like goose, with lots of dumplings. I think the Czechs eat more dumplings than anyone else in the world.

CHRIS: That sounds fine. Shall we walk or get a taxi ...

(*Later, in the restaurant*)

CHRIS: . . . and that was the best meal I've had for ages. It was a great idea to come here.

INGRID: Yes, I've really enjoyed it. Chris, how worried are you about the American competition?

CHRIS: They may not be as good as they think. We have a lot of very high quality up-to-date equipment as well. We'll see. I've got nothing to lose, anyway.

Colloquial terms

how did you find it? (6) what was your impression of it?
bourbon (48) American whisky
date (52) the person you are meeting, usually romantically
pals (54) friends
clinch a deal (58) finalize a contract
got it sewn up (58) got it settled; got it finalized
pretty good (60) fairly good

A2 Focus on structure—Comparatives and superlatives

1 How big is the new hospital in the other suburb compared with Praha-Dejvice?
2 How big are the hospitals in the provincial capitals?
3 How does the hospital at Praha-Dejvice compare with the other two new ones in Prague?
4 How do the new ones compare with the old ones?

A3 Focus on function—Comparing quality

Chris is trying to sell Plastech products. What does he say about

1 the range of products?
2 quality?

Focus on function—Describing processes

3 What happens in open-heart surgery?

A4 Vocabulary

Use the story to complete these sentences.

1 Chris thanks Mr Novotny for ______ ______ him so well.
2 You can bend some of the tubes. They are ______.
3 Plastech's sterilization process is excellent. It is ______ to ______.
4 The quality control is ______-______. It is really excellent!
5 The American hasn't signed any contracts yet. He hasn't ______ ______ ______.
6 The Pelikan is good for ______ ______.
7 The Czechs eat a lot of ______.
8 Plastech isn't the only firm trying to do business in Prague. There is some American ______.

9 Chris tells Ingrid that Plastech produces equipment which is modern and good. it is ______ ______, ______-______-______ equipment.

10 Chris may be lucky or unlucky, but Plastech haven't got any business in Czechoslovakia yet, so he's got ______ ______ ______.

Section B Extension work—Grammar practice

Comparatives and superlatives

Is it the biggest of your new hospitals?
There's one which is the same size
There are two which are much bigger
I would like to hear about something that's more sophisticated
. . . a machine which does the same job as the heart and lungs

The endings **-er** and **-est** are added to
(i) all adjectives that have only one syllable
(ii) all adjectives that end in **-y** (Note the spelling, for example, happy, happ**ier**, happ**iest**.)

more and **most** are used with
(i) most adjectives with two syllables
(ii) all adjectives with more than two syllables
(iii) all adjectives ending in **-ing** and **-ed**
(iv) all adverbs ending in **-ly**

Usually we say: **as** cold **as** ice; but sometimes, for example: it's not **so** big **as** I thought. Note that **different from** means **not the same as**.

B1 Fluency practice

Answer the questions below. Use the words in the brackets to help you.

1 Do all of the tubes have the same specifications? (*strong; flexible*)
2 How do the hotels in the suburbs compare with the ones in the city centre? (*modern*)
3 How do your inspection schedules compare with your competitors'? (*tight*)
4 Your competitors have a wide range of products, haven't they? (*wide*)
5 What job does the machine do in open-heart surgery?
6 Do the Czechs eat a lot of dumplings?
7 Compare the advantages and disadvantages of going from Europe to New York by plane and by boat.

B2 Free stage

Choosing a holiday

Look at the chart below and make 10 statements about these

holidays, comparing them for cost, standard of accommodation, time spent travelling, and other points

	Holiday A	Holiday B	Holiday C
Time	10 days	14 days	14 days
Destination	Paris	South of France (touring)	Istanbul
Accommodation	**Hotel	*Hotel	****Hotel
Transport	Coach (6hrs)	Coach (18hrs)	Train (26hrs)
Price	£420	£400	£500
Other points	2 meals per day	3 meals per day Guide available	3 meals per day Bathroom all rooms Guide

Section C Extension work—Functional areas

C1 Explaining a process

Look at the pictures which show how cans of soup get from the warehouse to the supermarket shelf. Explain:
(a) the system in 1960
(b) the new system

The system in 1960

The new system

Getting cans of soup from the warehouse to the supermarket shelf

Here is some vocabulary to help you.

boxes/cartons	shelf	to push
tins	forklift truck	to label
warehouse	container	to load
trolley	price	to stack
by hand/manually	assistants	to stamp
stack	to carry	

Now look at the pictures again and compare the two systems.

C2 Consolidation

You are trying to sell your car. A potential buyer is asking you questions about it. Complete the conversation and practise it with a partner.

BUYER: My present car does 8 litres to 100 kilometres. Is this car as economical?

YOU: ....

BUYER: Is it true the maximum speed is 110kph?

YOU: ....

BUYER: Mmm. I've heard these cars aren't very reliable.

YOU: ....

BUYER: Are they really? Anyway, there's a similar one at the garage down the road and it's £300 cheaper.

YOU: ....

Section D Listening work

D1 Structure exercise—Comparatives and superlatives

Medipraha are making their own evaluation of the medical products on the market. Look at the table below, and use the information to compare the Plastech product with the American one. Answer the questions you will now hear on the tape.

Example: How do they compare for strength?
The Plastech product is stronger.

	Plastech	PRH (USA)	DW (Germany)	CCMCS (USSR)
Strength	***	**	****	***
Flexibility	****	***	**	*
Smoothness	****	***	***	**
Price	$5 per unit	$4 per unit	$5 per unit	$3 per unit
Discount	10%	15%	17½%	—
Guarantee	5 years	3 years	3 years	2 years

(*The stars indicate product rating—the more stars the better the product.*)

You will then compare all the products, choosing the best each time.

D2 Story extract—Focus on function

Listen to the extract from the dialogue. Then listen and repeat.

D3 Listening for information

Chris tells Mr Tyborski about the strong points of Plastech products and explains how they are sterilized. Study the list below of some of the words he uses.

Equipment used in the compounding of materials

endotracheal tube a tube which goes inside the breathing passage in the throat
to buff to polish, to make smooth
to bevel to give a sloping edge
flange a projecting collar
to weld to join together by heat
ethyline oxide a gas used for sterilizing

Now listen to the tape and make notes about:
(a) the buffing process—why? how is it done?
(b) welding—what method? what advantages?
(c) sterilizing—how?
(d) testing and checking
(e) distribution

Use your notes to answer the questions you will hear.

Section E Group work

Many inventions

The following expressions are often used in advertisements for products sold by mail order, that is, when the customer writes to the seller to order the goods, and receives them by post.

Promotion and persuasion
New! Revolutionary! Unique! Amazing! Improved!
Now you can . . .
Easy to use.
No more problems with . . .
As advertised on TV.
Recommended by (experts, mountaineers, etc)
Ideal gift/present.
Satisfaction guaranteed.
Strong. Rustproof. Lightweight.
Are you . . .? Then . . .
For the first time.
Faster/cheaper/better than ever before.
Best ever.
Second to none.
First class quality.
Better than normal/conventional/well-known brands.

Payment
Special offer!
New low price!
Only £____.
Prices slashed (=reduced)!
From £____. (=this is the minimum price for the basic model with no extras)
£3 each or two for £5.25.
75p p & p (=packing and postage, an extra charge)
Carr (=carriage, the cost of transport)
CWO (=Cash with Order, you must send the money)
COD (=Cash on Delivery, you pay when you have received the goods)
Money back } if not satisfied
Full refund }

Now look at the following advertisements and see how many of these expressions you can find. What other expressions are used to persuade the reader to buy?

SAVE YOUR FEET!
TAKE IT EASY WHILE YOU WAIT!

Carry-Seat

The walking stick that converts to a seat

BUS QUEUES, SHOPPING, STATIONS, SPORTING EVENTS

Are you tired of standing around?
THEN TAKE A CARRY-SEAT.

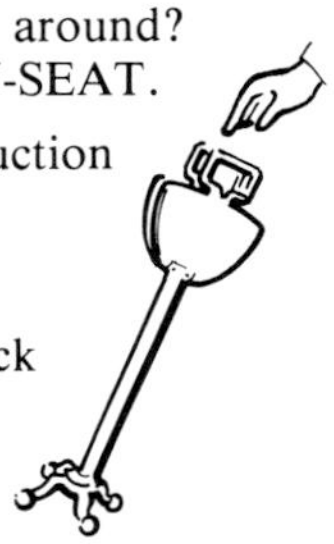

Strong aluminium construction
Rubber feet will not slip

£12.50 + £1.80 p&p

Satisfaction or money back

INDOORS OR OUT

Only 1kg.

LUCY EMMA ENTERPRISES
LYMINGE KENT CT18 8JA
0303-862599

Don't throw away old soap! Turn it into new!

ONLY £1
plus 25p p&p
or 2 for £1.80

IDEAL GIFT Money back guarantee
C.W.O. to Dexter and Barnes
Manor Road, FOLKESTONE

MAGIC WINDOW CLEANER!

AS SEEN ON TV!

First time in Britain

Clean both sides at once.

- Cleans and polishes both sides of your windows
- Child-easy to use
- Best ever labour-saving device
- Top quality
- Made to last

JAMES RENNIE WAREHOUSES
Foster House, Waste Lane
Manchester 12. 061-224-1933

£4.95 + 95p p&p.

The New Revolutionary Wallpainter

AS SEEN ON T.V.

NO MORE • Drips • Leaks • Splashes

UNIQUE TWIN-ROLLER SYSTEM

ONLY £7.99 + p&p.

Brighten up your home quicker than ever before!

ORDER NOW
MONEY BACK IF NOT DELIGHTED

Ideal as a gift for the proud home owner!

C.W.O. to BRONWEN HOUSEWARE
30 Birch Grove MANCHESTER 14

Prompt delivery

Strong lightweight extension handle

Now work in pairs or groups of three. Each pair must devise, and then promote by advertising slogans, diagrams and pictures, or any other means you can think of, one of the following:

1. A garden or kitchen tool.
2. Something to make motoring safer.
3. A desk-top device for making office work easier.
4. A piece of equipment for increasing physical fitness.
5. Something which is now done by microchip technology, but which previously needed people.

Finally, write a paragraph comparing your product to existing models or methods and showing that it is superior to them.

Reminder of key points in Unit 6

Functional areas

Comparing quality and performance

They're better equipped than the older ones.
a wider range
a process that is second to none
the best possible quality
We make these to specific requirements.
The quality control is first rate.
more reliable than anything else on the market

Explaining processes

The heart is disconnected while ...
... a machine which does the same job as ...
The flange and tube are welded together.
The finished products are checked again.
They are sent to the packaging and despatch departments for labelling and distribution.
blister packs
This is done by hand.

Structure: Comparatives and superlatives

—Some must be stronger than others.
—That was the best meal I've had for ages.
—They may not be as good as they think.

Unit 7

Structure:	Conditional 2
Functional areas:	Bargaining Contractual arrangements

The story so far: After his visit to the hospital, Chris met Mr Novotny and told him about Plastech's products, in particular the equipment for open-heart surgery. They arranged to meet again the next day, after Novotny had spoken to his colleagues. Chris then had dinner with Ingrid, who had met a rather confident American salesman from a company competing with Plastech.

Section A Dialogue and language work

A1 Guided listening

Read these questions before you listen to the story.

1 How big is the order?
2 Is there a problem about delivery?
3 Why will Chris add 3% to the price?
4 The main negotiations are over two points. What is the second?
5 After making the deal Chris rings his office again. Why?

Dialogue

(*Next morning, Chris is at the Medipraha office again.*)

NOVOTNY: ... Mr Telford, my colleagues and I are very impressed by the quality of your samples, and we may be able to give you a trial order. We have prepared a list of the items in which we are interested. Now, let me ask you—if we placed a firm order with you, when could you deliver the goods?

CHRIS: Could I see the list please? (*He reads the list.*) I see, Mr Novotny. This would amount to about £200,000.

NOVOTNY: Could you deliver in one month?

CHRIS: The whole consignment?

NOVOTNY: Yes.

CHRIS: I wouldn't be able to guarantee that, Mr Novotny. I must phone my head office. I think eight to ten weeks would be a more realistic estimate, for all this.

NOVOTNY: I don't think we could accept that, Mr Telford. How about part shipment? Could you deliver half the quantity in three to four weeks and the rest, shall we say, by July 20th?

CHRIS: Yes, I think so. Provided you didn't insist on a penalty clause covering those dates.

NOVOTNY: No, we wouldn't do that. Now, about payment. Your prices are quoted in sterling. How would you require payment?

CHRIS: This is our first business with you, Mr Novotny. Normally we would require you to open a confirmed and irrevocable Letter of Credit in England.

NOVOTNY: We didn't have to do that for the Germans, and I don't think your American competitors would insist on it, if we gave them the business.

CHRIS: I don't know about them, Mr Novotny, but we could accept payment by Bill of Exchange.

NOVOTNY: Payable at sixty days after sight?

CHRIS: Oh no, Mr Novotny, we would require payment at sight.

NOVOTNY: That may be acceptable. And your prices are FOB London. How much more would the CIF price be?

CHRIS: By road to Czechoslovakia, about 3% more. Do you agree?

NOVOTNY: It's less work for us, certainly, and it sounds reasonable. But let us consider the very important question of discount. What can you offer us?

CHRIS: I can offer you $7\frac{1}{2}$% on our published price.

NOVOTNY: Oh, Mr Telford, you can't be serious. You must do better than that. The Germans have given us 20% in the past.

CHRIS: Then they must be inflating their prices somewhere else. I can try to get you a 10% quantity discount. Would that be acceptable?

NOVOTNY: Yes. With one proviso. That if we placed any further orders within one year they would receive at least the same discount.

CHRIS: We don't usually make that kind of concession, but ... Mmm. I'd have to clear that with my boss. It's 8.30 in England at the moment. If I phoned now we'd have an immediate answer.

NOVOTNY: You're welcome to use the phone in the next office, Mr Telford.

(*Chris telephones London, then returns to Novotny's office.*)

NOVOTNY: Then we are agreed, Mr Telford. The list as specified, 50% in four weeks, the rest by July 20th. CIF London less 10%, payment in sterling, by Bill of Exchange payable at sight. And though we need not put it in the agreement, you will do your best to deliver a large part of the shipment immediately.

CHRIS: That's correct, Mr Novotny, and thank you, for myself and on behalf of my company.

NOVOTNY: Thank you, Mr Telford. And now we will have a little something in celebration ...

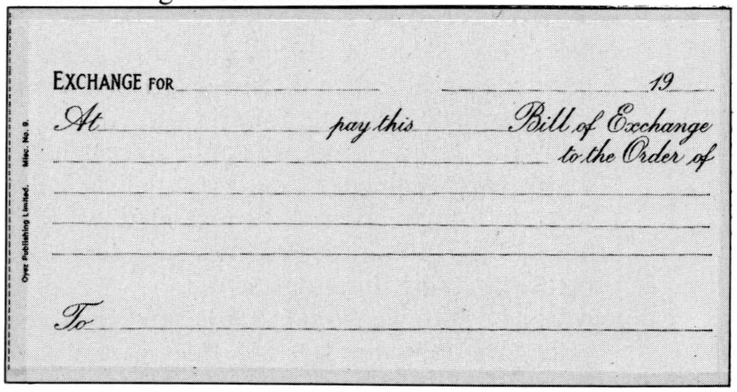
EXCHANGE FOR ______ 19__

At ______ pay this ______ Bill of Exchange to the Order of

To ______

Oyez Publishing Limited. Misc. No. 9.

(*The telephone rings.*)

SALLY: Mr Richardson's office.

CHRIS: Sally, Chris Telford, in Prague. Tell Tom to go ahead and get the stuff on the road *as soon as possible*. Last night, if he can! We mustn't make any mistakes now. And tell him I didn't have to go to $12\frac{1}{2}\%$.

SALLY: Yes, I will. And well done, Chris.

CHRIS: That'll show them we mean business. Thanks, Sally. Oh, and keep me in the picture, won't you? I'm off to Vienna tomorrow.

SALLY: I will, don't worry ...

Colloquial terms

with one proviso (45) on one qualifying condition
to clear that with my boss (49) to get his agreement
a little something in celebration (62) a drink
the stuff (66) the products; the goods
show them we mean business (70) show them we are serious
in the picture (71) informed; up-to-date

A2 Focus on structure—Conditional 2

This is often used for discussing possible, but not definite, arrangements. In his negotiations with Chris, Novotny asks several questions containing the idea, '*if* we signed a contract with you ...' What does he ask about the following?

1 Delivery times
2 Payment
3 The CIF price
4 Discounts on future orders

A3 Focus on function—Bargaining

1 Novotny is not happy about Chris's estimate of eight to ten weeks for delivery. What does he suggest? How does Chris agree?
2 What argument does Novotny use against an irrevocable Letter of Credit?
3 Novotny accepts a discount of 10%, but not unconditionally. What does he ask for?

Focus on function—Contractual terms

4 What do they finally agree about
(a) delivery dates?
(b) terms of payment?

A4 Vocabulary

Use the story to complete these sentences.

1 The Medipraha people are very ______ ______ the Plastech samples.
2 It's a large order. It would ______ ______ about £200,000.

3 Eight to ten weeks for delivery would be a more ______ ______.
4 Perhaps half the quantity, a ______ ______, could be delivered in three to four weeks.
5 How would Plastech normally require payment from a new customer? By ______ ______ ______ ______ ______ ______.
6 Plastech can't accept a delay in payment of the Bill of Exchange. They want ______ ______ ______.
7 Does Novotny agree to a 10% discount? Yes, with one ______.
8 Plastech will try to deliver a part shipment immediately. They will ______ ______ ______.
9 Chris thanks Mr Novotny ______ ______ ______ his company.
10 He wants progress reports, so he asks Sally to ______ ______ ______ ______ ______.

Section B Extension work—Grammar practice

Conditional 2

If we placed a firm order with you, when could you deliver the goods?
Your American competitors wouldn't insist on it, if we gave them the business

Like conditional 1 (see unit 3), conditional 2 may refer to either the present or the future. We use it for discussing unlikely situations or possible, but not definite, arrangements. It is often used in negotiations.

In the first example above, the arrangement is not yet definite. In the second example, the situation is unlikely. Both are used in a negotiating context.

B1 Fluency practice

Two managers are discussing whether or not to invest in more capital equipment. One is in favour of the idea, the other is against. Here are their reasons.

In favour

More equipment ▶ More goods ▶ Lower unit price ▶ Lower price ▶ Bigger market share ▶ More profit ▶ Happy share-holders.

Against

More equipment ▶ Bigger premises ▶ Higher overheads ▶ Cash flow problems ▶ Production difficulties and unhappy customers.

Now you produce their arguments. Work in pairs, one in favour of the idea, the other against.

Example: 1 If we bought more equipment we would produce more goods.
2 If we produced more goods . . .

B2 Free stage

A friend has been offered a job with a large company in London. At present he has his own small business in a seaside town. He is 40 years old. His interests are music, gardening and golf. He has two children of school age and his wife enjoys her part-time job.

Work in pairs or small groups and, using the information below, make a list of five reasons why he should take the new job, and five reasons why he should say 'No'. Begin each of the reasons like this:

<table>
<tr><td rowspan="3">If he</td><td rowspan="2">took the job,</td><td rowspan="3">he</td><td>could/couldn't . . .</td></tr>
<tr><td>would/wouldn't be able to . . .</td></tr>
<tr><td>lived in London,</td><td>would/wouldn't have to . . .</td></tr>
</table>

	Present job	London job
Salary	£10,000 per annum	£17,500 per annum
Job responsibility (number of staff) (budgeted turnover)	 6 £80,000	 24 £500,000
Pension	—	70% company, 30% employee
Private health insurance	No	Yes
Prospects	Fair	Excellent
Holidays	6 weeks per annum	4 weeks per annum
Travelling time (self) (family) Cost of living	 10 minutes (car) 15 minutes (on foot) £X	 40 minutes (underground) 10 minutes (bus) £X + 10%

Section C Extension work—Functional areas

C1 Bargaining

Listen again to some key phrases used in the Medipraha negotiations. Now complete them below.

I wouldn't be able to . . .
Eight to ten weeks would be . . .

I don't think ...
Provided you didn't ...
Normally we would require ...
We could accept ...
I can offer you ...
I can try ...

Now, work with a partner and try to reach agreement in the following situation. One of you is a buyer, the other is a seller.

Information for the buyer

You want to buy 1,000 cameras.
Ideally you want
(a) not to spend over £50,000
(b) payment to be in Italian lira
(c) delivery in two weeks

Information for the seller

You want to sell 1,000 cameras.
Cost price (to you) was £45 per unit and you want to make as much profit as possible.
Normal retail price is £60. Ideally, you want payment in US dollars, Deutschmarks or Swiss francs.
It will be difficult to deliver in less than one month.

Contractual arrangements

Draw up a 'contract' for your camera deal on the lines of the agreement below. Write it out on a separate piece of paper. Both parties must sign to show that you are agreed.

An agreement between ____________________

hereinafter called the purchaser, and

____________________, hereinafter called

the vendor.

Under the terms of this agreement the purchaser agrees to buy (*number/type of article*) from the vendor at a price of (*amount*) per unit. The total price of (*amount*) to be paid in (*currency*) on receipt of the above items.

The vendor agrees to deliver the total consignment on or before (*date*).

Signed: ____________ **Signed: ____________**

for the purchaser **for the vendor**

Date:

C2 Consolidation

A salesman is talking to a potential buyer. Complete the conversation, and practise it with a partner.

SALESMAN: ....

BUYER: I'm sorry, that's far too low. We want 15% off list price.

SALESMAN: ....
BUYER: No. We want to pay in pesos.
SALESMAN: ....
BUYER: All right then, if you accept $12\frac{1}{2}\%$.
SALESMAN: ....
BUYER: Sixty days? Yes, we can accept that.
SALESMAN: ....

Section D Listening work

D1 Structure exercise—Conditional 2

Chris and Mr Novotny are negotiating. You are Mr Novotny. Ask Chris about discounts on each of the products below and make a note of his replies.

Example: Number One
NOVOTNY: *What discount would you give us on 500 FG 24s?*
CHRIS: We'd give you $12\frac{1}{2}\%$ if you paid in sterling.

Now you ask about these products.

1 500 × FG 24
2 300 × FG 42
3 500 × FG 15
4 FT range

Now answer a colleague's questions with the information you have just received from Chris.

Example: What about FG 24s?
They'd give us $12\frac{1}{2}\%$ if we paid in sterling.

D2 Story extract—Focus on function

Listen to the extract from the dialogue then listen and repeat.

D3 Listening for information

An exporter is talking about her experiences of bargaining with Comecon countries. Look at the list of points below. Then listen and makes notes on these points.

1 FTO
2 FTO negotiators
3 Hard currency/local currency
4 Buy-back deal
5 Advantages to Comecon
6 Full documentation
7 Problems with this
8 Penalty clause/delivery dates
9 Overall costs

Then use your notes to answer the questions you will hear.

Section E Group work

Bargaining: Buses to Cuba

First turn to page 98 in the group work information section at the back of the book and read the information about Comecon and Cuba in the UK banks' market intelligence reports.

Now form groups of four or six people, of whom half are representatives of Chorley Motors UK, and half are members of Trancom, Havana.

Situation: Representatives of Chorley Motors are in Havana at the invitation of Trancom, a foreign trade organization of the Cuban government. Trancom want to buy buses and tractors. Chorley motors naturally want to get the business, but there is some hard bargaining to do first.

The exercise has a preliminary stage for information, and four or five bargaining stages:
Preliminary stage: When the groups and sub-groups have been chosen, the teacher will give an information sheet to all the Trancom members, and another one to the people from Chorley motors. These give details of the deal your organization would like to make. Study your information sheet carefully (probably as homework), but make sure that nobody from the other side sees it.

Stage 1: Meet together with your colleagues from Trancom or Chorley Motors. Make sure you all know what your position is and what you want from the deal. Decide provisionally what concessions you might be prepared to make.

Stage 2: Meet the other side and negotiate. This meeting should be chaired by a member of Trancom, who are hosts. Trancom should state their requirements first.

Stage 3: Confer with your colleagues again and decide what your position is, in the light of the negotiations you have carried out already.

Stage 4: Meet the other side again and finalize the deal if possible. Remember that if no agreement is reached, then *everyone* has failed.

Stage 5: (Optional, or for people who could not be given roles). Write an individual report to your Head Office or, as a reporter, to your newspaper, describing the negotiations that took place, what the result was, and making any suggestions about how business might be done better in future.

Reminder of key points in Unit 7

Functional areas

Bargaining

Provided you didn't insist on ...
Ten weeks would be a more reliable estimate.
I wouldn't be able to guarantee that.
Could you deliver in one month?
What discount can you offer us?
I can offer you $7\frac{1}{2}\%$ on published prices.
We don't usually ..., but ...
Then we are agreed.

Contractual agreements

a firm order
the whole consignment
a confirmed and irrevocable Letter of Credit
a Bill of Exchange payable sixty days after sight
CIF London, payable in sterling
a 10% quantity discount

Structure: Conditional 2

—If we placed any further orders, they would receive the same discount.
—If we placed a firm order, when could you deliver the goods?

Unit 8

Structure:	Reported speech
Functional areas:	Public speaking Reporting

The story so far: After a good deal of negotiation about terms and conditions, Medipraha have given Chris an order for about £200,000 worth of goods to be delivered in two part shipments. Chris has promised to try to effect delivery of the first part shipment well in advance of the contract date, and has passed shipping instructions to Head Office. He and Ingrid are now at the IHA conference in Vienna. Chris has taken some time off to hear Ingrid give her speech.

Section A Dialogue and language work

A1 Guided listening

Read these questions before you listen to the story.

1 What is Ingrid's talk about?
2 What is the main idea in her talk?
3 Is the talk a success? Why do some people object to her ideas?
4 Chris has a problem. What is it?

Dialogue

CHAIRMAN: Fellow delegates, ladies and gentlemen, it gives me great pleasure to introduce Dr Ingrid Fowler, of the International Health Agency. Dr Fowler has had many years' experience in her field in India, Indonesia and East Africa. The title of her talk is *Water, Society and Health.* She tells me she will gladly answer questions at the end of her talk. (*Applause*)

INGRID: Thank you, Mr Chairman, thank you. Ladies and gentlemen, as the Chairman said, I will answer questions later; but if anything urgent comes up during my talk, I shall try to deal with it on the spot.

In her book, *Progress for a Small Planet*, Barbara Ward says, and I quote, 'There will never be a conserving society if it is largely made up of careless and selfish citizens.' I am often reminded of her words in my work in developing countries. For 'conserving society' read 'healthy society', and the same is true. But I want to make one other important point. I say to you that there will never be a healthy society made up of ignorant citizens. People must know how to be unselfish and responsible. This is especially true of the provision of new water supply

systems. Many schemes which have been carefully planned and generously financed have failed. And why? Because the people they were designed for did not know how to benefit from them. This is a question of education, as much as of medicine. Let me give you an example . . .

FIRST VOICE (*interrupting*): Dr Fowler, do you think that social change can be brought about quickly?

INGRID: Can we come back to that point later? The question is much too general at this stage. May I continue? When I was working in Uttar Pradesh the Government said it would send . . .

. . . So in conclusion, let me say again, what people need, everywhere, is a reliable and plentiful water supply. But it must be available for everyone; and everyone must know how to profit from it. It's no good building a dam, if you deprive a whole valley of water. It's no good digging irrigation ditches if they only spread disease. Most of all, it's no good doing anything at all, if it only benefits the big landowners. Unless the whole community benefits, your food programmes, your land clearance schemes, your water systems, will come to nothing. My final word is, technical change without social transformation can achieve nothing permanent. This is something we must never forget. Thank you. (*Applause*)

CHAIRMAN: Dr Fowler, on behalf of everyone here, I would like to thank you for a most stimulating talk. Now, has anyone got any questions? Yes?

SECOND VOICE (*indistinctly*): Mr Chairman, on a point of information, is Dr Fowler speaking on behalf of the IHA, or are her views only her own?

CHAIRMAN: Dr Fowler?

INGRID: I'm sorry, I didn't quite catch the question.

CHAIRMAN: The delegate asked if you were speaking on behalf of the IHA, or whether your views were only your own.

INGRID: My views are my own. They are of course known to the IHA.

CHAIRMAN: Are there any other questions?

FIRST VOICE: Dr Fowler, I asked you earlier if you thought social change could be brought about quickly, and you said the question was much too general. I'd like to put it to you again now, if I may.

INGRID: It depends what you mean by 'quickly'. Once policy decisions are made and the objective is clear, I believe there need be very little waste of time.

THIRD VOICE: Dr Fowler, you said that technical change without social revolution could achieve nothing. That sounds to me like political interference. What right have you to engage in political activities in other countries?

CHAIRMAN: Can I just come in here? I don't think Dr Fowler said or implied anything about political activity.

INGRID: Thank you, Mr Chairman. No, I didn't. I am a doctor. I have no political message whatever. Furthermore I did not use the word 'revolution'. I said 'transformation'.

THIRD VOICE: What's the difference?

INGRID: The difference is perfectly clear. Let me put it this way. By 'transformation' I mean . . .

(*After the conference*)

CHRIS: Oh, hello Ingrid, how did it go? I liked your speech, but I'm afraid I missed the questions afterwards, I had to go and talk business. Somebody told me you had a bit of an argument. According to him somebody practically accused you of being a revolutionary. Is that right?

INGRID: Yes, he did. He was quite rude about it.

CHRIS: However, my friend also said that the Chairman supported you, and that you put the fellow firmly in his place.

INGRID: Well, I hope so. But it just shows, you have to be careful what you say.

CHRIS: Yes indeed. Now then . . .

PA: Attention please. Will Mr Telford, representative of Plastech, England, please come to the information desk. Mr Telford, please . . .

CHRIS: Oh, excuse me a moment. Don't go away!

CLERK: Mr Telford? We've received a telex message for you from England. It arrived a few minutes ago.

CHRIS: What's this, then? (*reading the telex*) 'Medipraha order delayed by Belgian customs Ostende, early arrival Prague impossible.' Oh, good Lord! 'May be delayed beyond contract date, stop. Contact Medipraha and request delay of up to two weeks, phone me soonest, stop. Richardson.' Oh no, it's too much . . .

Colloquial term

put him in his place (82) made him appear inferior

A2 Focus on structure—Reported speech

1 How does the chairman repeat a question for Ingrid?
2 How does he interrupt a questioner?

Chris wasn't there for the questions.

3 How did he find out what had happened?
4 How much did his friend tell him?

A3 Focus on function—Public speaking

1 How does the Chairman open the meeting and introduce Ingrid?
2 While she is speaking, Ingrid is asked a question about social change. How does she delay answering it?
3 When she is about to finish her speech she repeats and reinforces her main argument. What does she actually say?
4 How does the Chairman thank her and invite questions?
5 Listen again to the opening of Ingrid's speech, when she talks about new water supply systems. Pick out the main point she makes.
6 Listen again to her closing remarks. What is the main point she makes?

A4 Vocabulary

Use the story to complete these sentences.

1 Ingrid will try to ______ ______ anything urgent on the spot.
2 Indonesia and Ethiopia, for example, are not highly industrialized. They are ______ ______.
3 The question about social change was too ______ to answer during the talk.
4 People need a lot of good, clean water. The water supply should be ______ and ______.
5 Ingrid asks a questioner to repeat because she didn't quite ______ ______ ______.
6 Someone who attends a conference is a ______.
7 Chris wants to know if the talk was a success. 'How ______ ______ ______?'
8 He wasn't there for the questions. He ______ them.
9 Ingrid was not upset by the aggressive questioner. She put the fellow firmly ______ ______ ______.
10 Tom Richardson wants to speak to Chris urgently, so he telexes '______ ______ ______'.

Section B Extension work—Grammar practice

Reported speech

'The question is much too general' (direct speech)
You said the question was much too general (reported speech)

'Is Dr Fowler speaking on behalf of the IHA, or are her views only her own?' (direct speech)
The delegate asked if you were speaking on behalf of the IHA, or whether your views were only your own (reported speech)

The words inside the quotation marks ('...') are the exact words spoken. When speech is reported to another person, there may be two sorts of change.

(i) *Reference*: The nouns and pronouns may change, as in the second example above (**Dr Fowler** changes to **you**, **her** changes to **your**). Also, if the time and place are different, other changes will be necessary. Look at these examples:

'I will meet you here'

He said he would meet me there

'I want to do it now'

She said she wanted to do it then/straight away

In these examples, **here** changes to **there**, **now** changes to **then** or **straight away**.

(ii) *Tense*: If the reporting verb, for example, **say**, is in the present, present perfect or future tense, then the tense of the verb(s) in the direct speech does not change. If the reporting verb is in a past tense, then the tense of the verb(s) in the direct speech also changes to the past. Look at these examples:

'I want to discuss it first'

He says he wants to discuss it first (present)

He said he wanted to discuss it first (past)

Note that after the reporting verb **that** is always possible but never necessary. It is used more often in written English.

Say and **tell** are the most important reporting verbs. Remember that after **tell** there must always be a mention of the person who hears the words spoken. For example:

She tells me she will gladly answer questions

Barbara Ward says, and I quote, 'There will never ...'

Reported questions change reference and tense in the same way. There is no auxiliary **do** and the word order is the same as for statements. They repeat question words like **what** and **where**. In yes/no questions they include **if** or **whether**. Look at these examples:

Where do you live?

He asked me where I lived

Can you speak French?

She asked him {if / whether} he could speak French

B1 Fluency practice

You are a journalist at the conference. Put the following sentences into reported speech, beginning '*The Chairman said ...*'

Example: 'Dr Fowler has worked in Indonesia.'
The Chairman said that Dr Fowler had worked in Indonesia.

1 'She is a well-known expert on water supply problems.'
2 'She has just come back from a project in Malaysia.'
3 'She's going to talk about irrigation.'

4 'She will answer questions at the end of her talk.'
5 'She has raised some very interesting points.'

Put the following questions into reported speech, beginning *'One of the delegates asked . . .'*

Example: 'Are you speaking on behalf of the IHA?'
One of the delegates asked Dr Fowler if she was speaking on behalf of the IHA.

6 'Do you think social change can be brought about quickly?'
7 'Have you worked in Africa?'
8 'Are you a political agitator?'
9 'Will you explain your point about irrigation ditches?'
10 'Can I take you out to dinner?'

B2 Free stage

Study the phrases below, which you can use instead of **say** and **tell** to report speech.

made the point that . . .	concluded by saying . . .
began by saying . . .	went on to say . . .
pointed out . . .	added . . .
emphasized . . .	told the audience . . .

Now use these phrases to write a connected report of Ingrid's speech, in which she said the following:

'I will try to deal with urgent questions on the spot.'
'There will never be a healthy society made up of ignorant citizens.'
'People must know how to be responsible.'
'Many schemes which have been generously financed have failed.'
'This is a question of education.'
'It is no good doing anything if it only benefits the big landowners.'
'Technical change without social transformation can achieve nothing.'

When the report is finished, read it aloud to the group.

Section C Extension work—Functional areas

C1 Public speaking and reporting

Listen again to the tape and note
(a) how the Chairman opens the meeting and introduces Ingrid
(b) how Ingrid begins her speech and how she finishes it
(c) how the Chairman thanks her and asks for questions
(d) how the questions are asked and how the Chairman interrupts a questioner

Now work in small groups. You are at a conference. One of you is the Chairman, one of you is the speaker, and the others are delegates. The delegates should take notes during the speech:

Chairman

Introduce the speaker. He/she can talk on any subject for two to five minutes.

Speaker

Give your talk, with a proper introduction and conclusion.

Chairman

Thank the speaker and ask for questions.

Delegates

Ask questions.

Speaker

Answer or delay the delegates' questions.

The delegates must now
(a) give a short summary of what the speaker said
(b) write a short report of the talk, using the phrases already practised in exercise B2 above.

C2 Consolidation

A scientist is giving a speech about laser beams. Complete the exchange below, and then practise it.

CHAIRMAN: ....

JAMES RENNIE: Thank you, Mr Chairman. I'd like to begin my short talk on 'Laser Beams' by giving a brief history of their development.

QUESTIONER A: ....

JAMES RENNIE: That's an interesting question, but I'd like to deal with the whole field of the medical application of laser beams later, if I may . . .
(*much later*)
. . . and so I hope I have been able to give you an idea of the latest developments in the field.

CHAIRMAN: ....

QUESTIONER B: Yes, I have a question. Could Mr Rennie tell us what he thinks about . . .

Section D Listening work

D1 Structure exercise—Reported speech

Use the expression *Did anyone ask about . . . ?* to ask questions about the points below.

Example: Social change
Did anyone ask about social change?

1 Social change
2 Water supply systems
3 Irrigation schemes
4 Dam building

Now use the expression *What did she say about . . . ?*

Example: Education
What did she say about education?

5 Education
6 Technical change
7 Political activity
8 Financial aid

Now look at the extracts from Ingrid's speech in exercise B2 above. Use the information to answer the questions you will hear on the tape.

Example: What did Dr Fowler say about urgent questions?
She said she would try to deal with them on the spot.

D2 Story extract—Focus on function

Listen to the extract from the dialogue. Then listen and repeat.

D3 Listening for information

Chris is talking to some of the delegates after Ingrid's speech. Take notes of what the delegates from each country said about the following points:

1 Argentina—the important issues
2 Greece—Ingrid's talk
3 The Philippines—Ingrid's talk
4 Kuwait—money
5 Windward Islands—problems
6 USA—projects in developing countries
7 Mozambique—water supply

Now you are Chris. Use your notes to answer the questions Ingrid will ask you.

Section E Group work

Microchips and employment

First turn to page 100 in the group work information section at the back of the book and read the three extracts concerning new technology.

Now look at part of a report of a conference on the subject of microchips and employment, (on the next page).

Form groups of four or five people. One of you is the speaker, one is the Chairman; the others can make the interruptions and ask the questions. You must decide exactly what the speakers said, and be able to enact the proceedings as if you were the speakers.

1. The Chairman opened the conference and welcomed the delegates. He introduced the first speaker, the British scientist Dr Lionel Tipton, now working with Siliconstant Incorporated in San Fernando, California. Dr Tipton is a pioneer in microprocessor development and was optimistic about the future.

2. Leslie Potter asked the Chairman why Dr Tipton was optimistic.

3. The Chairman said Dr Tipton could explain that himself.

4. Dr Tipton thanked the Chairman and began by saying that he was very happy to be present. He went on to say that he was optimistic because this was the beginning of a new age.

5. Pat Cheetham said that was what they had said after they dropped the first atomic bomb.

6. The Chairman called order. He reminded the meeting that delegates should not make general observations, or speak direct to one another, but should address all their remarks to him, as Chairman.

7. Dr Tipton made the point that the atomic bomb had been a weapon of war, but the microchip was not. He added that even so, atomic energy used peacefully had brought great benefits to the human race. All great technological advances created prosperity and jobs, he told the audience, and this was an advance as important as the invention of the steam engine.

8. Steve Underdown told the Chairman he was a shop steward who had studied industrial history. Everyone knew that machinery driven by steam had put a lot of people out of work.

9. The Chairman said he would not tolerate any more interruptions. He reminded the audience that Dr Tipton had come to tell them what microtechnology could do in the 20th and 21st centuries, not to discuss the past.

10. Dr Tipton thanked the Chairman and pointed out that he was well aware that sudden and drastic change could cause trouble, but he was confident that with proper planning such trouble would be avoided. If Mr Underdown wanted to keep things as they were he must be a Conservative, which was a strange attitude for a Trade Unionist. If they would allow him to continue...

11. In conclusion, Dr Tipton restated his main points. The unions had already accepted automation in industry. Microchips would take things further and faster, that was all. Boring, dirty and dangerous jobs could be abolished, and people could turn to jobs which were satisfying, enjoyable and useful to society - in leisure industries, in information, in social service. This tremendous change was happening whether they liked it or not. He hoped they would, like him, be excited and challenged by the opportunities of a new tomorrow.

12. The Chairman thanked the speaker and asked for questions.

13. Pat Cheetham said word processors were already destroying thousands of secretarial jobs. Where were all the young women to go - back to cooking and looking after children?

14. Dr Tipton said that on the contrary he expected a lot of women to go into management.

15. Leslie Potter said that was quite impractical for most women, and declared that it was quite clear that a lot of jobs would disappear. He asked what would happen to the people who were put out of work.

16. Steve Underdown said they would have to be paid not to work, or be retrained for other jobs.

17. Leslie Potter asked who would pay for that.

18. Dr Tipton said the Government would have to help, and he was confident that they would.

19. Pat Cheetham asked why Dr Tipton was working in California, if he thought so much about the British Government.

20. Dr Tipton said he liked America because people faced the future optimistically and were not frightened of new developments. He told the delegates to think of Japan.

21. Steve Underdown asked what Japan had got to do with the matter.

22. Dr Tipton said that Japan had invested more into microtechnology than any country in the world, proportionate to its size; and that it had the lowest rate of unemployment in the Western world.

23. Numerous delegates protested that Britain was not the same as Japan.

24. The Chairman said that we could still learn from them, nevertheless, just as one hundred years ago they had learned from us. He then said time was up, thanked Dr Tipton for his fascinating talk, and called on the next speaker.

Reminder of key points in Unit 8

Functional areas

Public speaking
Ladies and Gentlemen . . .
It gives me great pleasure to introduce . . .
. . . as the Chairman said . . .
Let me give you an example.
Can we come back to that point later?
So, in conclusion, let me say again . . .
On behalf of everyone here I would like to . . .

Reporting
Somebody told me . . .
According to him . . .
She didn't imply anything about . . .
You said that . . .
Did anyone ask about . . .?
What did she say about . . .

Structure: Reported speech

—I asked you earlier if you thought social change could be brought about quickly, and you said the question was much too general.

Unit 9

Structure:	Present perfect/past simple contrast
Functional areas:	Dealing with an emergency Customer relations

The story so far: Ingrid has given her talk about water supply systems and their social context. During the talk she had to deal with some rather unfriendly questions. Chris has been looking for useful business contacts. He has just received a telex from England telling him that the Medipraha order has been delayed in Belgium.

Section A Dialogue and language work

A1 Guided listening

Read these questions before you listen to the story.

1 How does Mr Novotny react to Chris's request?
2 What caused the delay in Ostende?
3 Chris makes two suggestions to Tom Richardson. What are they?
4 Is Chris pleased at the news that Tom gives him in the morning?

Dialogue

(*The telephone rings.*)

OPERATOR: You're through, caller. Go ahead.

CHRIS: Mr Novotny?

NOVOTNY: Ah, good afternoon, Mr Telford. I was just leaving. What can I do for you?

CHRIS: Mr Novotny I'm sorry, but I have some bad news. The truck carrying your order was stopped in Belgium last night, and it hasn't been released yet.

NOVOTNY: Stopped, Mr Telford? What has happened?

CHRIS: Apparently there has been some trouble with the Customs in Ostende. Mr Novotny, I deeply regret this, and I know how inconvenient it is, but could you possibly accept a delay in delivery for the first half of the order? Say up to July 7th?

NOVOTNY: Two weeks? Oh, I don't think that's possible. One moment, I must speak to Mr Tyborski. (*a few minutes later*) Mr Telford, I'm sorry, we cannot accept the delay. The terms of the contract are quite clear—delivery was promised by June 23rd. We have been relying on you, Mr Telford. I hope that was not a mistake?

CHRIS: No, Mr Novotny, of course not. You can depend upon us to find a satisfactory alternative. We're very anxious that our relationship should get off to a good start, and we'll do everything in our power to get the problem sorted out at once. But it isn't really our fault that the Belgian Customs have acted like this.

NOVOTNY: I appreciate your difficulties, Mr Telford, but may I point out that I started importing twenty-two years ago and no one has ever suggested to me before that in a CIF contract the transport is not the responsibility of the seller.

CHRIS: Good heavens, Mr Novotny, I wasn't trying to evade our responsibilities, I assure you. Please don't worry. I'll speak to my Head Office and ring you in the morning, if I may?

NOVOTNY: Please do, Mr Telford. I shall be waiting anxiously.

(*on the telephone*)

RICHARDSON: Richardson.

CHRIS: Tom, it's Chris Telford in Vienna. The Czechs won't accept any delay.

RICHARDSON: Oh damn.

CHRIS: Well, you can't blame them, Tom. What the hell has gone wrong in Ostende? It's a straightforward transit through Belgium, surely?

RICHARDSON: Unfortunately it's not just a customs problem. The police are involved too. Someone broke into the trailer on Ostende docks and the police have detained the driver for questioning. Then they found some error in the papers. It could take ages to sort out. Still, we're covered by insurance.

CHRIS: Insurance! But that's not the point, Tom. This is an important breakthrough. Can't we send a replacement cargo by air?

RICHARDSON: With the discounts you've been promising that would just about make sure we lost a fortune on it. Anyway, we haven't got the goods to send.

CHRIS: Well, aren't there any consignments we could divert? The monthly Australian order hasn't left yet, has it?

RICHARDSON: No, it hasn't, but I'm not going to break into that. For heaven's sake, Chris, you know the form. We don't upset an

old customer just on the off-chance of getting a new one. I switched a cargo from Toronto to Mexico three years ago. It was a disaster. I've never done it since.

CHRIS: But this is the chance of a lifetime, Tom. It's the best order we've had for years. And there could be plenty more.

RICHARDSON: Yes, and they could turn round next week and say sorry, nice to have met you, we're going back to the Americans. It's not on, Chris.

CHRIS: Well, I don't think it makes sense. The Australians always carry a lot of stock. You could fix it with them easily enough.

RICHARDSON: Look, Chris, I know how you feel, but don't try to tell me how to do my job. I've been exporting a lot longer than you have. I got my first order for Plastech when you were still in short trousers.

CHRIS: Oh, I'm sorry, Tom, I didn't mean that. (*pause*) You're right, of course. (*pause*) I'll get on to Novotny and tell him we can't do anything. You never know, he might be sympathetic.

RICHARDSON: I wouldn't count on it. (*long pause*) Look Chris, it's against all my principles, and I shall probably regret it, but as this one is rather special, I'll do what you ask. Or at least I'll try. I'll have to ring old Freeman in Sydney and put it to him personally.

CHRIS: Oh thanks, Tom, thanks a lot. That's terrific.

RICHARDSON: It's the middle of the night in Sydney, so I can't possibly reach him before 10 o'clock tonight. I'll do that and let you know first thing in the morning. I'll ring you at 5.30, that's 7.30 in Vienna. OK?

CHRIS: Yes. I won't contact Medipraha until I hear from you.

(*The telephone rings.*)

CHRIS: Telford.

RICHARDSON: Chris, Tom Richardson. You'll be glad to hear that Sandersons have agreed to a ten-day delay, so we can put together the items for the first half of the Prague consignment from their order, and despatch it right away.

CHRIS: Oh thanks, Tom, that's marvellous.

RICHARDSON: Right, so take these details down and pass them on to Prague right away, will you?

CHRIS: Have you fixed all the details already? But how on earth . . .

RICHARDSON: Oh, I pulled a few strings. Now, have you got a pen . . .?

Colloquial terms

oh damn! (39) *what the hell!* (40)	slang expressions of annoyance

A2 Focus on structure—Present perfect/past simple contrast

1 What does Chris actually say to Mr Novotny about the truck?

2 Why is Tom against diverting consignments? Does he often do it?
3 How does Tom stress that he is the man with experience in exporting?

A3

Focus on function—Dealing with an emergency

1 What reason does Richardson have for phoning Freeman rather than sending him a telex?
2 How will Plastech get the consignment for Prague? When will they send it?
3 What does Tom want Chris to do with the details? How did he get the problem sorted out with so little trouble?

Focus on function—Customer relations

4 Chris is very polite and apologetic when he gives Mr Novotny the bad news. What does he say?
5 He wants to reassure Mr Novotny that Plastech are a good company and will find a way to deliver on time. What does he say?
6 What is Tom Richardson's usual policy on switching cargoes to get new customers?

A4

Vocabulary

Use the story to complete these sentences.

1 The ______ of the contract are quite clear.
2 We're a reliable company. You can ______ ______ us.
3 We'll act fast to get the problem ______ ______.
4 Someone else made the mistake. It's not ______ ______.
5 This is the first order from Czechoslovakia. It's an important ______.
6 Chris wants to ______ some other consignments to Czechoslovakia.
7 This sort of opportunity doesn't happen very often. It's the ______ ______ ______ ______.
8 The Australians won't be short of supplies because they always ______ ______ ______ ______ ______.
9 Tom doesn't expect Novotny to be sympathetic. He says he wouldn't ______ ______ it.
10 Tom used his influence and his personal contacts. He ______ a ______ ______.

Section B Extension work—Grammar practice

Present perfect/past simple contrast

The truck carrying your order was stopped in Belgium last night and it hasn't been released yet

I switched a cargo from Toronto to Mexico three years ago. I've never done it since

I've been exporting a lot longer than you have. I got my first order for Plastech when you were still in short trousers

Look again at the notes on the present perfect in Unit 1.
The present perfect is used

(i) to say *how long*, usually with **since ...** or **for ...**
(ii) to say *at some time*, or to ask *at any time?*, but without stating the exact time
(iii) to say *how many times*

If further details are given, for example, *when, why, how* or *where* something happened, the past simple is used.

B1 Fluency practice

Put these sentences in either the present perfect or the past simple, using the words in brackets.

1 I ______ just ______ (*have*) some bad news.
2 Someone ______ (*break into*) the lorry this afternoon.
3 While they were checking, the police ______ (*find*) some errors.
4 I ______ (*be*) in exports for 22 years (and I'm still in exports).
5 I ______ (*be*) in exports for 22 years (and I retired in 1980).
6 ______ the Australian order ______ (*leave*) yet?
7 I ______ (*get*) my first order when you ______ (*be*) in short trousers.
8 I ______ (*work*) here since the office opened.
9 When ______ Tom ______ (*phone*) Chris?
10 It's 1am. Is Ingrid still up, or ______ she ______ (*go*) to bed?

B2 Free stage

Work in pairs. Ask your partner questions, so that you can complete the following parts of a questionnaire. Ask questions like these:

What's the name of your present company?
How long have you worked there?

	Name/Title	Number of years
Present company		
Position in company		
Previous company		
Previous position		

	Yes/No	If yes, number of years
College/ university		
Married		

Countries visited in last 12 months	Date	Length of stay	Reason for visit
1.			
2.			
3.			
4.			
5.			

Visits to:	Yes/No	If yes, number of visits	If yes, date of last visit
America			
Africa			
Middle East			

Section C Extension work—Functional areas

C1 Dealing with an emergency

How did Tom and Chris deal with the emergency? Who did they contact and why? How fast did they act to send the Prague consignment? How did Tom arrange things so quickly? Listen to the extracts on the tape.

Now you have a small crisis to deal with. Work in pairs.

> It is 5.30pm on Friday. You are just about to leave the office when you hear that a plane has unexpectedly been diverted to your local airport because of bad weather. The President of your company and his wife are aboard. All the first class hotels in the town are probably full because it is Gala Night at the Opera. What will you do?

Discuss the situation with your partner and decide on a plan of action.

Customer relations

What excuses did Chris give Novotny for the delay? How did Novotny react? How did Chris reassure him? What did he promise to do? Listen to the extracts on the tape.

Now work in pairs and practise this language. One of you is a farmer, and the other is a customer. The farmer should look at the information in the box on the left, the customer should look at the information in the box on the right. First, the farmer telephones the customer.

Farmer

You are a fruit grower. Phone one of your customers and explain why the apples he ordered will be delayed. Choose your reasons —bad weather —lorry has broken down —trees have been attacked by birds —all labour is needed to pick pears Try to pacify your customer and offer solutions to the problem.

Customer

You have ordered 100 crates of apples from this farmer. You need them in two days to make fruit pies. Any delay will be extremely inconvenient. It is the farmer's responsibility to deliver.

C2 Consolidation

Work in pairs and complete the conversation below between a sales representative (you) and a dissatisfied customer. Then practise it with your partner.

CUSTOMER: I have a complaint. Nearly half the items in the last consignment arrived damaged.

YOU: ....

CUSTOMER: Maybe the damage did happen at the docks, but it's still your responsibility to see that the goods are securely packed. I need replacements right away. My production line is being held up.

YOU: ....

CUSTOMER: Next month! This is an emergency. I can't possibly wait as long as that.

YOU: ....

Section D Listening work

D1 Structure exercise—Present perfect/past simple contrast

Use the checklist below to help you answer the questions you will hear on the tape.

Example: Has Chris phoned Novotny?
Yes, he phoned him at 5.30.

D2 Story extract—Focus on function

Listen to the extract from the dialogue. Then listen and repeat.

D3 Listening for information

It is Wednesday 31st. Tom Richardson is phoning his Forwarding Agent about the dispatch situation for various orders. Listen to their conversation and complete the table below.

Destination	Date consignment received	Date consignment sent
AMERICA		

M	T	W	Th	F	S	Su
15	16	17	18	19	20	21
22	23	24	25	26	27	28
29	30	(31)	1	2	3	4

Now answer the questions you will hear on the tape, using the information from the table.

Section E Group work

Dealing with an emergency

Work in groups of six or eight people (T Bridgeman and B Dewar can be omitted if you prefer).

As this is an emergency, the essential thing is not to waste any time. Speed is essential. See if you can make all the necessary decisions in 15–20 minutes—30 minutes is certainly too long. However, it is essential that everyone knows exactly what he has to do when the meeting closes.

The teacher will allocate roles.

The situation

You are the management of an airline in Hong Kong (5 Boeing 707's, flying to Bangkok, Manila, Tokyo, Osaka, Djakarta, Taipei and Perth).

It's Sunday morning. The time is 10.45. Half an hour ago your flight SE2 to Manila blew a tyre on take-off, failed to get airborne, and ran off the runway into Hong Kong Harbour.

Emergency services were on the spot immediately. First reports indicate that one person has been killed (possible heart attack?) and about half the 103 passengers are injured to a greater or lesser extent.

The injured are now on their way to hospital. The runway has been cleared for use. Your plane is still partly visible in shallow water near the end of the runway.

Mr Bluck has called an emergency meeting in the airline office at the airport and luckily most of the airline management has already arrived. The people at the meeting are as follows:

Mr Duncan Bluck	Managing Director
J Dick	Traffic Manager (in charge of day-to-day operations)
D Cheetham	Planning Manager (in charge of schedules)
C Graham	Sales Manager
B Dewar	Chief Accountant
B Delaney	Engineering Manager
B Clarke	Public Relations and Advertising Manager
T Bridgeman	Management Trainee

Instructions

Make a list of everything you must do, short term and long term, to deal with this emergency and minimize its effects on the company. Decide who should deal with what, and the order of priority of jobs for everyone.

Mr Bluck must make sure that everyone knows exactly what they should do when the emergency meeting breaks up!

Points to consider

Passengers: how many injured/hospital liaison/onward flights
Luggage: recovery/compensation
Plane: present situation/liaison with airport authority/damage/insurance
Public relations: announcement/contacting relatives/what are passengers entitled to?
Planning: rescheduling planes/crew/maintenance/new timetables/charter?
General: see that everyone involved knows what is happening/keep the company in business as effectively as possible in the short term, and start making longer term arrangements.

Reminder of key points in Unit 9

Functional areas

Dealing with an emergency
There's been some trouble.
The police are involved.
... get the problem sorted out.
What's gone wrong?
Can't we ...?
It could take ages.
I'll have to ...
First thing in the morning.
Right away.

Customer relations
I know how inconvenient it is, but ...
You can depend on us.
We'll do everything in our power.
It really isn't our fault.
I appreciate your difficulties, but ...
You could fix it easily enough.
You'll be glad to hear that ...
I pulled a few strings.
I deeply regret this.

Structure: Present perfect/past simple contrast

—I started importing twenty-two years ago.
—What has gone wrong in Ostende?
—I switched a cargo three years ago and I've never done it since.

Unit 10

Structure:	Conditional 3
Functional areas:	Analysing results and making forecasts Congratulations and thanks

The story so far: When he heard of the delay in Belgium, Novotny was displeased. He told Chris that Medipraha would not accept any delay, so Chris had to make alternative arrangements. After some argument, Tom Richardson agreed to contact a customer in Australia and try to persuade him to accept a delay in his order, so that the goods could be sent to Prague. Later he rang and told Chris the Australians had agreed.

Section A Dialogue and language work

A1 Guided listening

Read these questions before you listen to the story.

1 What does Ingrid give Chris before they say goodbye?
2 Richardson shows Chris two telexes. Are they good news?
3 What will Chris's next overseas trip probably be?
4 Why does he ring Fibak?
5 What do you think Chris is going to do this evening?

Dialogue

INGRID: Cheerio, then, and I hope everything goes well in Germany. When will you be back?

CHRIS: It all depends on our Frankfurt agent, really. Perhaps I could give you a ring next week.

INGRID: Please do; this number will always find me. And by the way—well done. Plastech should be very pleased with you.

CHRIS: Why, thank you. It's nice of you to say so.

(*Chris's visit to Frankfurt is busy but routine, and he returns to England at the weekend. On Monday morning he goes into the office to give his report.*)

CHRIS: Good morning, Sally. Mr Richardson in?

SALLY: Yes, he's waiting for you. I say, you've been busy, haven't you? Everybody's talking about you this morning.

CHRIS: Thank you, Sally, that's very nice of you.

(*The door opens.*)

RICHARDSON: Ah, it's the man of the moment. Come in. You'd better look at these.

CHRIS (*reading*): 'Plastech from Medipraha. Replacement cargo arrived in full Saturday morning third, stop. Entirely satisfied and grateful your efforts in difficult situation, stop. Provided no difficulty with second part shipment due 20th July will certainly place further orders from August. Novotny.' Well, thank goodness for that.

RICHARDSON: Yes, Chris, I'm quite prepared to admit you were right this time. If you hadn't argued so forcefully, I wouldn't have diverted the Australian stuff.

CHRIS: There won't be any problems with the second lot, will there?

RICHARDSON: No, we can manage that all right. As a matter of fact we can probably get that consignment clear from Ostende in a day or two, so we should be sitting pretty. All the same, here's the other side of the coin ...

CHRIS: Who's this from? Ah, Sanderson and Yule, in Sydney. (*reading*) 'Re your phone call 31st May we accept late arrival of June order but please understand this is an exceptional case and must not be regarded as a precedent, stop. We value our association but would remind you it is based on mutual respect and precise fulfilment of commitments on both sides.' Yes, I see. Oh Lord, Tom, if I'd known they would react like this I wouldn't have ...

RICHARDSON (*interrupting*): Oh, it's all right, they're just making their position clear. They don't mind really. Mind you, if I hadn't known old Freeman, or if I hadn't been able to speak to him personally, it might have been another story. I've done him a few favours in the past, now he's done us one. Next time it'll be our turn again. You know how it is in business, it's all give and take, really. Now, have you written a report?

CHRIS: Yes, I've got it here.

RICHARDSON: Fine. Well, Chris, this is quite a feather in your cap.

CHRIS: I was lucky, I think. The contact with Novotny was a useful break, but I've got a feeling the Czechs were looking for a new supplier to try. We got in touch with them just at the right time.

RICHARDSON: I must say, to be honest, the competition wasn't as stiff as I thought it would be. Why was that, do you think?

CHRIS: I'm not sure. Over-confidence, perhaps? If PRH had pushed harder we might have found it a lot more difficult.

RICHARDSON: Well, now we're in there we mustn't make the same mistake. We've made a good start and we ought to be able to build on it. We might get the lion's share of the market, if we play our cards right. Have you any immediate suggestions for the future?

CHRIS: I think I should go out there again soon. There's a lot going on, and I'd like to get a precise idea of their likely needs over the next year or two. Also in the short term there's a chance of something similar in Hungary that I'd like to follow up. One thing often leads to another, and with a bit of luck our long term prospects throughout the Eastern bloc could be very good. I've put it all in the report.

RICHARDSON: Right, I'll read it this morning and go over it with you later. And once again, Chris, congratulations. You did a grand job.

CHRIS: Thanks. And now I must ring and say thank you to Fibak.

(*on the telephone*)

FIBAK: Fibak speaking.

CHRIS: Mr Fibak, it's Chris Telford of Plastech here. I've just got back from Prague, where I met your friend Mr Novotny. He sends his regards.

FIBAK: Ah yes, Mr Telford, thank you. And was your trip successful?

CHRIS: Very. And I have you to thank for that. If you hadn't been so helpful, I would probably never have gone to Prague at all. You did me a very good turn, and I'm grateful. Can I give you lunch one day soon?

FIBAK: With pleasure, Mr Telford. I'm glad I was able to help and I'm very pleased that things went well.

(*on the internal telephone*)

CHRIS: . . . And last but not least, Sally, do you think you could try and get me Dr Ingrid Fowler, at the IHA, London?

SALLY: Just a minute. (*later*) They say she's gone to Guatemala for three years. Didn't she tell you?

CHRIS: No, she didn't. Well, what do you know? That's a bit sudden. I'm sure she'd have mentioned it, if . . .

SALLY: Never mind. Three years won't seem long if you keep yourself busy.

CHRIS: Oh, thank you very much. (*He rings off.*) Hm, I wonder. (*He picks up the phone again.*)

SALLY: Yes?

CHRIS: Sally, you remember you said you'd never been to the Pilgrims' House . . .?

The Pilgrims' House

Colloquial terms

sitting pretty (31) in a good position (for future business)
the other side of the coin (32) the opposite view
a feather in your cap (49) a great achievement
a useful break (52) a piece of good luck; an opportunity
the lion's share (61) the biggest part
if we play our cards right (62) if we act sensibly; if we do not make any mistakes
you did me a good turn (85) you helped me

A2

Focus on structure—Conditional 3

1 Tom is pleased that Chris pushed him to divert the Australian order. What does he say?
2 What difference did Tom's personal contacts make to the arrangements with Sandersons?
3 Why does Chris thank Fibak?

A3

Focus on function—Analysing results and making forecasts

1 Give two reasons why Plastech got the Medipraha contract.
2 How does Chris want to follow up this breakthrough? What are the prospects for Hungary? What about the Eastern bloc in general?

Focus on function—Congratulations and thanks

3 How does Ingrid congratulate Chris, and what is his reply?
4 What does Chris offer Fibak, and what is Fibak's reply?

A4

Vocabulary

Use the story to complete these sentences.

1 How is Chris going to contact Ingrid in London? He's going to ______ ______ ______ ______.
2 Was the visit to Frankfurt unusual? No, it was ______.
3 Everyone's talking about Chris. He's the ______ ______ ______ ______.
4 When the consignment is cleared from Ostende, everything should be all right and they will be ______ ______.
5 Sandersons will accept the delay this time, but it must not be ______ ______ a ______.
6 He has done us a good turn. It will be our turn next. Business is all ______ ______ ______, really.
7 PRH should have ______ ______ to get business in Czechoslovakia.
8 With any luck, Plastech should get a very big proportion, ______ ______ ______, of the market.
9 He will ______ ______ the report with Chris later.
10 Novotny was very helpful. He did Chris a ______ ______ ______.

Section B Extension work—Grammar practice

Conditional 3

If you hadn't argued so forcefully, I wouldn't have diverted the Australian stuff

If PRH had pushed harder, we might have found it a lot more difficult

Conditional 3 refers to the past. We call the conditions 'impossible' because we know what happened, and know that it cannot now be changed. We are thinking about something which was possible at the time, but which in fact did not happen. Chris says to Fibak, *If you hadn't been so helpful, I would probably never have gone to Prague at all*—but as we know, Fibak *was* helpful, and Chris *did* go to Prague.

B1 Fluency practice

Complete the sentences with the words in brackets.

Example: If Chris ______ (*not go*) to the party, he ______ (*not meet*) Ingrid.
If Chris hadn't gone to the party, he wouldn't have met Ingrid.

1 If Fibak ______ (*not give*) Chris the introduction to Novotny, it ______ (*be*) harder to do business with Medipraha.
2 Medipraha ______ (*not sign*) the contract if they ______ (*not be*) satisfied with the terms of payment.
3 Would Plastech ______ (*get*) the order if PRH ______ (*try*) harder?
4 What ______ (*happen*) if Plastech ______ (*not meet*) the delivery dates?
5 If there ______ (*not be*) trouble at Ostende, Chris ______ (*arrive*) in Frankfurt earlier.
6 Ingrid ______ (*tell*) Chris if she ______ (*know*) she was going to Guatemala.
7 ______ Chris ______ (*invite*) Sally out to dinner if Ingrid ______ (*not go*) to Guatemala?

B2 Revision exercise—All structures

Complete the conversations below, using the words in brackets where appropriate.

A Chris talks to Fibak before his visit to Czechoslovakia

CHRIS: I ______ (*work*) for a company which ______ (*make*) medical equipment.
FIBAK: You ______ (*ever go*) to Prague?
CHRIS: No, I ______.
FIBAK: The Czech Government ______ (*expand*) its medical services. They ______ (*build*) a lot of bigger, newer, ______ (*good*) hospitals.
CHRIS: That's interesting. If I ______ (*get*) an order there, it ______ (*open up*) a new market for us.

B After the visit

FIBAK: What was the trip like?

CHRIS: I ______ (*impress*) by the new hospitals. One ______ (*finish*) already, and another one ______ (*finish*) in two years' time.

FIBAK: Did the business go well?

CHRIS: I ______ (*must*) stay in Vienna an extra day because there were some problems, but otherwise everything went very ______ (*good*), and I ______ (*not have to*) stay very long in Germany.

FIBAK: You ______ (*tell*) earlier that you ______ (*meet*) an attractive and helpful lady doctor.

CHRIS: That's right, Ingrid Fowler. She ______ (*visit*) relatives while I ______ (*negotiate*) with Medipraha. She ______ (*give*) one of the ______ interesting speeches at the Vienna conference.

FIBAK: What ______ (*talk*) about?

CHRIS: She said that social problems ______ (*be*) very important in irrigation projects, and that such factors ______ (*become*) even more important in the future.

FIBAK: ______ (*see*) her since you got back to London?

CHRIS: No, unfortunately she ______ (*go*) to Guatemala for three years. She ______ (*leave*) three days ago.

FIBAK: Bad luck!

CHRIS: It certainly is. Still, I'm going to Hungary next month and if I ______ (*be*) lucky it ______ (*be*) the start of something big there. Thank you again for your help, Mr Fibak. If you ______ (*not give*) me the original information, we ______ (*not get*) the business with Medipraha.

Section C Extension work—Functional areas

C1 Analysing results and making forecasts

Tom Richardson congratulates Chris on the Medipraha deal. Listen again to the reasons Chris gives for the success of his trip.

Tom wants to follow up the breakthrough. He asks Chris for suggestions. Listen again to what Chris says.

Now form small groups. Each group is a marketing team. During a recent visit to Greece you met Dr Koulouki of the Commercial Department of the UK Embassy. He made the following points:

1. High technology equipment:
   Prospects are not very good at present because of shortage of cash. However, there will be a need for cardiac, diagnostic and ultrasound equipment in the future.
2. Disposables:
   The local manufacture of catheters and syringes does not meet demand and is not always of high standard. There is a preference for imported material and prospects are good in this area, provided that the price is competitive.
3. There are three new teaching hospitals in the future health-care programme for Greece, which should enhance the market potential for those suppliers who are by then established.

Use this information, your own knowledge and your imagination, to prepare a report on Greece under the following headings:

1 Existing and planned medical facilities
2 Contact
3 Local factors (e.g. economic situation)
4 Competition
5 Estimated potential
6 Suggested action

Present your report to the Sales and Marketing Manager (the teacher).

Congratulations and thanks

Listen again to the way Richardson congratulates Chris, and how Chris thanks Fibak. Now work in pairs and find suitable comments to make in the following situations.

1 You have run out of petrol on the motorway. It is raining. You haven't got any money. Your neighbour stops and gives you a lift to a service station, lends you £20 and takes you back to your car. You want to thank him.
2 Your neighbour has just won the Nobel Prize for literature and announced his engagement to a well-known literary lady. You want to congratulate him.

C2 Consolidation

You have just come back from the South American Trade Fair. Complete the conversation with your Sales Manager and then practise it in pairs.

SALES MANAGER: Did you get any ideas from the South American Trade Fair?

YOU: ....

SALES MANAGER: But is there really a good chance of breaking into that market?

YOU: ....

SALES MANAGER: Well, you seem very enthusiastic. What action do you suggest we take?

YOU: ....

SALES MANAGER: Hmm. I'll have to think very carefully about that.

Section D Listening work

D1 Structure exercise—Conditional 3

You are the Sales Manager of a company making tennis rackets. The first half of the year has been disastrous for you. You are having an unpleasant interview with the Managing Director. Look at the sales graph showing forecast and actual sales and at the calendar of events. Explain to the Managing Director what went wrong.

Example: The January figures were very disappointing. We only sold 2,000.
We'd've sold 3,000 if we hadn't had a strike.

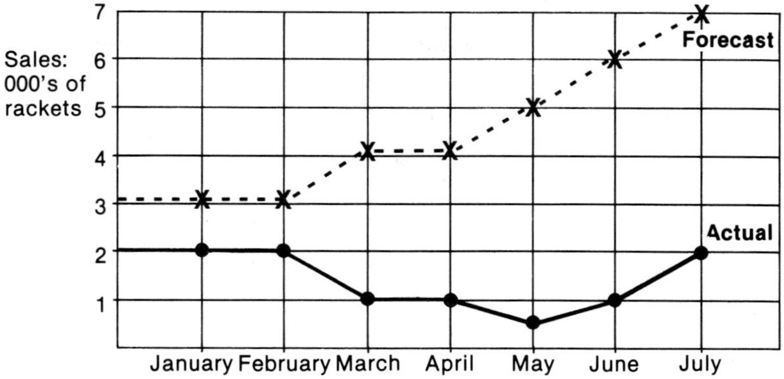

January	Strike
February	Shortage of raw materials
March	Fire in warehouse
April	Price rise
May	Distribution problems
June	Increased competition from Japan
July	Heavy rain

D2 Story extract—Focus on function

Listen to the extract from the dialogue. Then listen and repeat.

D3 Listening for information

Chris has arrived at the office to discuss his report with Tom Richardson. Look at Tom's checklist of questions and make a note of Chris's answers as you hear them.

Now you are Chris. Answer the questions you will hear on the tape, using your notes to help you.

Then take the part of Tom, and ask questions about the report, using the notes to help you.

Section E Group work

Hilldale Camping

Divide into groups of four. The teacher will give the members of your group the following names: Robin Lane, Arthur Collier, Pat Bullen and Val Ashfield. You are the Management Committee of Hilldale Camping, a private limited company which makes and sells camping equipment. It is January 16th, and you are meeting to consider last year's results and the prospects for the coming year. Your teacher will give you individual material and information. Study it in preparation for stage 1 of the project. You will each have:
(a) a copy of a newspaper article
(b) a graph with statistical information
(c) a letter or internal company memo
(d) some handwritten notes of your own

Stage 1: Use the material you are given by the teacher to prepare a 5–10 minute survey for the other members of the Committee, as follows:

Robin Lane	Analysis of last year's results: Favourable factors.
Arthur Collier	Analysis of last year's results: Unfavourable factors.
Pat Bullen	Forecast for the next 12 months: Favourable factors.
Val Ashfield	Forecast for the next 12 months: Unfavourable factors.

Make sure your colleagues know what you are talking about and understand exactly what you mean. You can give them written notes, draw pictures on the blackboard, or use any other means you choose.

Stage 2: When stage 1 is completed, discuss the overall situation as a group for 10 minutes and decide, on the basis of what you know, whether or not you believe that the company will do better in the next year than in the previous year. Choose one of your members to give a 3-minute talk to the class explaining your conclusion.

Stage 3: After your spokesperson has given his 3-minute talk, the other members of the class (including the teacher) will ask questions or make comments. These must be dealt with by the other three members of the Committee.

Stage 4: In the light of what you have heard, decide together what steps you will take to optimize the company's sales this year and in the future.

Here is some general information about Hilldale Camping:

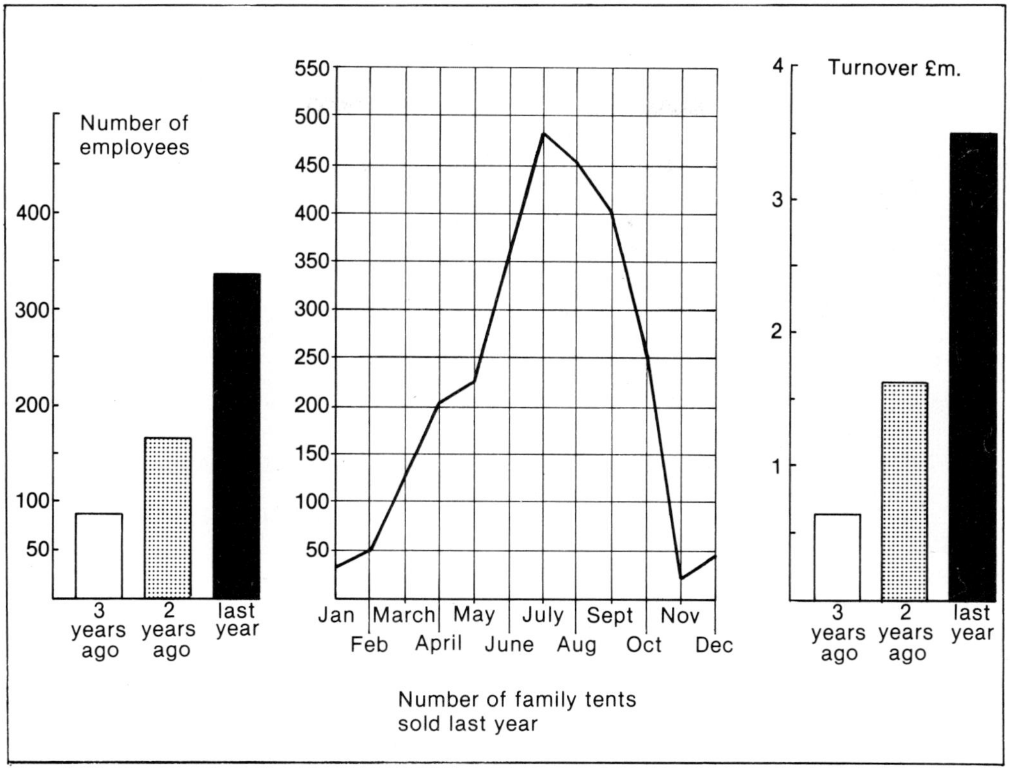

Colloquial terms used in Section E

economic headaches financial problems
a masterstroke a very good idea; a great success
snowed under very busy indeed
beat up attacked violently and injured
climbing on the bandwagon joining a successful movement in order to share in the profits
they must look to their laurels they must work hard to maintain their superior position
the shape of things to come the way in which things will happen in the future
to shop around to go to a lot of different suppliers, comparing prices, quality, etc
jerry-built built badly with low quality materials
it makes dismal reading it is discouraging to read
it hasn't sunk in yet most people have not yet realized the real situation
word will get around everyone will hear about it
things look black it seems that there will be trouble
to know what the score is to be fully informed
starting from scratch beginning again; going back to the starting point
old hat no longer fashionable

Reminder of key points in Unit 10

Functional areas

Analysing results and making forecasts

There won't be any problems.
We can probably ...
I've got a feeling that ...
What's the first priority?
What would happen if ...?
We mustn't make the same mistake.
We ought to be able to ...
There's a chance of ...
Our longterm prospects could be good.

Congratulations and thanks

Well done!
It's nice of you to say so.
You did me a very good turn.
I'm glad I was able to help.
I'm pleased things went well.
Congratulations. You did a grand job!

Structure: Conditional 3

—If you hadn't argued so forcibly, I wouldn't have diverted the Australian stuff.
—Would Medipraha have cancelled the order if we hadn't delivered on time?

Group work information section

Unit 3

Information for the travel agent

Hotels

Hotels in Copenhagen:

Kronenborg...	£50 per night
Imperial	£35 per night
Funen	£25 per night

Hotels in Hamburg are all booked up this week except for luxury accommodation at the **** Four Seasons, from £90 per night.

Air

Journey time from city centres to airports is one hour. Check-in time is 45 minutes before take-off.

Daily flights, outward only (Return flights are at exactly the same times.)

(a)	London	*dep* 10.00	Copenhagen	*arr* 11.50	British Airways
	London	*dep* 16.30	Copenhagen	*arr* 18.10	Scandinavian Airways
(b)	London	*dep* 07.00	Hamburg	*arr* 08.45	British Airways
	London	*dep* 13.00	Hamburg	*arr* 14.45	Lufthansa
(c)	Hamburg	*dep* 08.00	Copenhagen	*arr* 08.45	SAS/Lufthansa
	Hamburg	*dep* 13.00	Copenhagen	*arr* 13.45	SAS/Lufthansa
	Hamburg	*dep* 18.00	Copenhagen	*arr* 18.45	SAS/Lufthansa

Fares, Economy Class Single (Return fares are twice the single fare.)

London—Copenhagen	£120.00
London—Hamburg	£82.50
Hamburg—Copenhagen	£42.50

Sea

London—Harwich Dock, one hour by rail, with direct connection to ferry.

SAILING TIMES

HARWICH—HAMBURG—HARWICH MS KING CLAUDIUS	1 JAN—26 SEPT 25 OCT—31 DEC	27 SEPT—24 OCT
Depart Harwich (Parkeston Quay)	12.30	13.30
Arrive Hamburg (St. Pauli Pier)	09.30	09.30
Depart Hamburg (St. Pauli Pier)	13.30	13.30
Arrive Harwich (Parkeston Quay)	09.00	10.00

Harwich-Hamburg Fares

Single Fares (return fares double) meals on board not included.

PASSENGERS	1 JAN–30 JUNE 1 SEPT–31 DEC	1 JULY–31 AUG
Adults	£40.50	£46.75
Children under 14 years	£21.00	£24.50

Children under 4 years free if no berth is required. If berth is required, child fare is payable in addition to berth supplement.

The Company reserves the right to restrict the number of passengers travelling without accommodation supplements.

SUPPLEMENTS FOR ACCOMMODATION

	INSIDE with shower & toilet	OUTSIDE with shower & toilet
2 berth suite–per suite	—	£72.00
Deluxe 2 berth, per cabin	—	£57.50
Cabin for single occupancy	£30.50	£32.00
Cabin for double occupancy per berth	£17.00	£18.50
4 berth cabin, per berth	£12.00	£12.75
Family cabin, per cabin (Min. 3 fare-paying passengers)	£25.00	£28.50
4 berth cabin C/D deck (no sh/toilet) per berth	£7.00	—
	1 JAN–30 JUNE 1 SEPT–31 DEC	1 JULY–31 AUG
Pullman berth (no shower or toilet)	£4.50	£6.50

Rail/Sea/Rail

Through booking from London.
For fares, see note on map.
The Dover—Ostende crossing takes $3\frac{1}{2}$–4 hours.

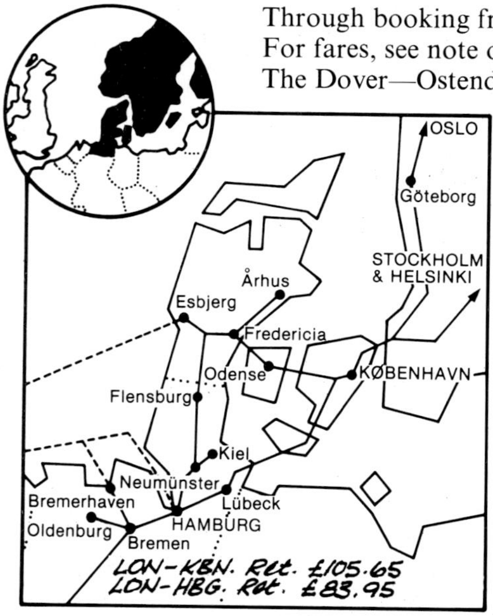

London	dep 09.44	13.44	20.44
Dover	11.40	15.45	22.45
Ostende	17.53	21.03	05.23
Hamburg	03.20	08.29	14.19
Copenhagen	arr 09.09	14.09	19.40
Copenhagen	dep 09.40	16.55	21.10
Hamburg	15.35	22.50	03.15
Ostende	00.15	09.29	13.14
Dover	04.10	12.45	17.20
London	arr 06.48	15.02	19.35

Vehicle Security

- **Roadside assistance**
- **Spare Parts service**
- **Vehicle recovery**
- **Assistance following illness**
- **Legal assistance and customs duty**
- **Emergency credit**
- **Continental emergency services**
- **Comprehensive service booklets**
- **Bail bond (for Spain)**

Local help

1. If, because of an accident, breakdown or fire to or of your vhicle you are unable to use it, we will pay

up to £200 for the AA to arrange the **location and despatch of any necessary spare parts**–including communications expenses and any necessary local collection costs–(but excluding the cost of the parts themselves, repairs and any import dues) for accident, breakdown or fire occurring overseas.

up to £50 for **emergency repairs including towage** to the nearest garage where necessary, **and storage**, to enable you to continue your journey in your vehicle (but excluding the cost of any parts themselves). Cover applies 'from home to home'.

2. If your vehicle breaks down on the Continent you may normally obtain **free roadside assistance** from an AIT (Alliance Internationale de Tourisme) patrol.

Spare parts guide

3. In case you need spare parts for your vehicle we provide the **Car Components Guide**, a 12-language guide designed to help you identify the particular component you require and overcome language difficulties.

If local help is not available

4. We provide the AA's own **Continental Emergency Service** for the whole of Europe at Boulogne-sur-Mer. This is the foremost English speaking service for motorists on the Continent. There is a **free phone service** (libre appel) for you when travelling in France if you need to use this service. This facility together with the location of the Emergency Service actually on the Continent normally gives far quicker access to help than schemes where it is necessary to first telephone the UK in an emergency.

Additionally, by special arrangement with the Dutch Motoring Club (ANWB), the ANWB's English-speaking Emergency Services in Mendrisio on the Swiss/Italian border, and at Barcelona in Spain, will help you.

Vehicle Recovery

5. If you cannot use your vehicle for eight hours or more because of illness and there is no other qualified or competent driver in your party or because of an accident, breakdown, theft, or fire, to or of your vehicle, and it cannot be repaired economically when overseas, **or**

if your vehicle is stolen and not recovered until after you and your party have returned home, we will pay

all necessary costs for **towage** to the nearest garage or place of safety and **up to £20 for storage PLUS**

all necessary costs for the AA to arrange recovery of the vehicle to your own home or to an appointed repairer (but excluding return sea passage and repair charges and service charge where appropriate—see note below).

Cover now applies 'from home to home'. Where your vehicle is recovered from overseas and arrangements are made by the AA for its transhipment you will normally be able to recover the cost of the return sea passage.

Note A service charge of £75 is payable for the recovery from overseas of vehicles five years old or over where this is necessary as a result of breakdown **unless** the Vehicle Security Supplementary Premium is paid—see Cost on page 12.

6. If your vehicle is being repaired overseas following accident, breakdown, theft or fire and the work will not be finished in time for your scheduled return journey, and in the meantime you and your party have returned home, we will pay

up to £250 for necessary additional hotel and travel expenses, including Green Card charges, for one person to collect the vehicle when the repairs are completed.

Assistance following illness

7. If the one and only qualified and competent driver in the party is declared **medically unfit** to carry on driving we will pay **up to £750** for a chauffeur (provided at the AA's discretion) to drive your vehicle and passengers home. Cover applies 'from home to home'.

Legal assistance and customs duty

8. If you are involved in an accident or motoring offence overseas we will pay **up to £250** for lawyers' fees (but excluding fines), subject to the prior approval of the AA.

This is in addition to the free legal advice to which AA members are entitled from many affiliated motoring organisations on the Continent.

9. If your vehicle is stolen or completely destroyed when overseas and you are therefore unable to export it as required by regulations and so become liable for Customs charges and taxes, we will meet **all necessary costs** or otherwise protect you against any Customs Duty claims which arise in these circumstances.

Emergency Credit

10. In case you are faced with unexpected costs following a vehicle breakdown or other emergency overseas, we provide **approximately £154** in AIT Credit Vouchers. These vouchers may be used to pay for most repair accounts, towing, medical expenses, technical reports, legal assistance, and in some circumstances, air tickets to return home. AIT Credit Vouchers are not valid for hotel expenses or car hire (but see Touring Security), and they cannot be used in the UK, the Isle of Man, the Republic of Ireland or the Channel Islands.

The amount of any bill settled by means of AIT Credit Vouchers must be repaid on receipt of an account from the AA. The rate of exchange applied will be the one operating on the day of settlement by the AA. A transfer charge of £2.50 is made per settlement.

11. In case one of your party has to return home urgently from overseas as a result of an emergency OR if your vehicle is being recovered by the AA we provide an Emergency Repatriation Voucher for £200 which can be exhanged for passenger tickets to return home by an AA agent or specified offices of Wagon Lits on the Continent.

You will have to repay the cost of the tickets on your return, but you may be entitled to make a claim under Touring Security if you have taken this cover.

Bail Bond

12. If you have an accident in Spain it can have serious consequences, so the AA has arranged through Lloyd's the provision of a £1,500 Bail Bond for a premium of £2.00 for purchasers of Vehicle Security. Further details are given on page 24 of this brochure, and on the AA 5-Star Service Proposal Form.

NOTE:

THE SERVICES WHICH HAVE A RING ROUND THEM, LIKE THIS

are only available for members of the AA.

Unit 7 Information for 'Buses to Cuba'

A Doing business with Comecon

Trading with Comecon is definitely not for the faint-hearted. Successful penetration of their markets depends mostly on being known and on having a good reputation.

Comecon countries consider foreign trade to be too serious to be left to businessmen, in the western sense. The tough professional negotiators in the Foreign Trade Organizations have generally been in their jobs for years. They tend to be very cautious. Decisions must be arrived at collectively, and they do not like taking risks.

British exporters should be prepared to enter into 'compensatory' or 'buy-back' contracts. Comecon countries often ask for these because they are short of hard currency. In these contracts the exporter supplies equipment and know-how, and takes the product of the buyer in part payment. This means that after some negotiation the FTO might come back and say, 'We like your product, we want to buy it, but we do not have the hard currency. Will you take zlotys ... or jam?'

Trade negotiations provide Comecon countries with a great deal of free technical information, as they all insist on having the fullest possible documentation from their potential supplier. It is not easy to provide enough information to clinch a deal without giving away too many secrets.

Pricing has to be worked out extremely carefully; but price is not the only thing which determines the profitability of a deal. There are usually penalty clauses for late delivery, and part of the FTO bargaining technique is to try to secure the earliest possible delivery dates. Rash promises of quick delivery times is a sure way of losing money.

There are other problems. Sometimes the buyer insists on guarantees of satisfactory performance, and this may be affected by the quality of materials supplied locally, over which the supplier has no control. In the case of complicated 'buy-back' deals, moreover, it is difficult for the British exporter to ensure the quality of the parts or the material which he agrees to accept in payment for his products.

B Cuba

	Cuba	UK
Area (square miles)	44,206	94,214
Population (1979)	9.7 million	55.8 million
GNP (1979)	£7,163 million (estimated)	£189,990 million
GNP per head (1979)	£739 (estimated)	£3,404

Exchange rate: Cuban pesos 1.683=£1 sterling. (February 1981)

Cuba shares full membership of the Council for Mutual Economic Assistance (CMEA or Comecon) and continues to rely on aid from the Soviet Union. 1980 was disappointing, but the hard currency trade deficit has decreased. Disease affected the tobacco and sugar crops, and full recovery is not expected immediately.

US trade embargoes are still in force. During 1980 there was mass emigration, as more people became dissatisfied with the low standard of living.

To improve productivity, measures were introduced during 1980 which are very different from the original principles of the revolution. Inefficient workers can now be sacked. Different wages can now be paid, so that the most productive receive more. State socialism is relaxed in other areas. Farmers who meet their production quotas are now allowed to sell their surplus on open markets. Many services, formerly obtained from the government, can now be provided privately.

To increase foreign exchange earnings, entry requirements for tourists have been relaxed. The authorities encourage tourism, as they receive money from import duties and from the currency which visitors spend in special stores.

According to the Five Year Plan, the industrial sector will expand in the near future. The development of the country's nickel resources, which represent 10% of the total known world supply, will play a major part.

Cuba's economic performance and prospects depend on sugar. She normally produces about 7% of total world output. The major purchasers of Cuban sugar are the Soviet Union in particular, and the rest of Comecon in general.

Reliable economic information is difficult to obtain. There is usually a trade deficit with the West. Foreign trade is supported by direct subsidies and trading agreements with Comecon countries, especially the USSR. An agreement to increase Cuban–Soviet trade by 50% by 1985 was recently signed, which means that Cuba will co-operate even more closely with the Soviet Union. Without Russian aid on this scale, the economy would collapse.

The greatest obstacle to the development of the economy is still the trade embargo imposed by the US, formerly Cuba's major trading partner. There is little prospect of any fundamental change in the relationship between the two countries.

Unit 8

Information for 'Microchips and employment'

A From the *Sunday Monitor*

From a recent survey on employment it was discovered that a large majority of the people in Britain (70%—80%) believe that new technology, above all the microchip, is replacing and will continue to replace people with machines. Gloomily and pessimistically, they look forward to a jobless future.

B From *The Revolutionary Microchip*, by Bernard Broad

"There is general agreement that we must use the chip wherever we can, and soon. But to one vital question, 'Will microtechnology create more new jobs than it destroys old ones?', the answer differs widely depending on who you ask. Many people just do not know, and say so freely, but there are in general two opposing schools of thought. On the one hand the optimists — industrialists, economists and some politicians — say that all technological advances in history have created more, different, and often more satisfying jobs, and that microtechnology will be no exception. On the other hand the pessimists (they prefer to be called 'realists') — union leaders, experts on microtechnology itself and politicians of different beliefs — say that in future so many jobs will be done more efficiently and more cheaply by microchips that there will inevitably be massive unemployment and, as a result, serious social upheaval. Different surveys have reached very different conclusions. One has predicted a million new jobs in the Western world by 1987, another says that **ten million** jobs will be lost in the same period. Everyone seems to agree that even those jobs which do not disappear will be radically changed, and that 'job security', as it has long been known, is disappearing fast."

C A '10-point plan on technology agreements', drawn up by the Trades Union Congress as a starting point for discussions with employers.

1 Management must not introduce new technology without union agreement.
2 Unions will collaborate in negotiations and help each other with technical know-how.
3 All information must be shown to the unions before decisions are taken.
4 No redundancies. Planned re-location of staff. Technology to be used to improve job and living standards.
5 Workers will be trained, and retrained for new jobs, as necessary.
6 Working hours should be reduced and overtime should be abolished.
7 Existing pay structures should be maintained.
8 Unions will be consulted about systems design. Personal privacy of employees must be guaranteed.
9 Health and safety standards must be established.
10 Joint union/management teams will be set up to review progress.

Glossary of business, technical and medical terms

(The number in brackets refers to the unit in which the word first appears.)

Anaesthetic system (5) System which makes the patient unconscious before an operation
Bankrupt (3) Financially completely ruined
To bevel (6) To give a sloping edge
Bill of Exchange (7) Order to a bank to pay a sum of money on a given date
Blister packs (5) Plastic air-tight containers
Blow moulding (5) Method using air pressure to form articles from plastic
To buff (6) To polish, to make smooth
Buy-back deal (7) A contract where part payment is made in goods, not money
Calibrated (5) Marked with measurements
Cardiac, diagnostic and ultrasound equipment (10) *cardiac*—to do with the heart; *ultrasound*—a method of using very high frequency sound waves to 'see' inside the body and record a 'picture' on a monitor
Cash flow (7) Money coming in and going out of the company
Catheters (1) Carefully manufactured plastic tubes used for medical purposes
CIF (7) Cost Insurance Freight. The seller pays all charges up to the port of delivery.
Comecon (2) The Eastern Europe trade group, roughly equivalent to the Common Market (the EEC) in Western Europe.
Confirmed and irrevocable Letter of Credit (7) See 'Letter of Credit' below. *Irrevocable* means the credit can't be withdrawn once the seller has been informed.
DDR (3) Usually known as East Germany
Endotracheal tubes (5) Tubes going inside the breathing passage in the throat
Ethyline oxide (6) A gas used for sterilizing
Export Credit Guarantee (2) A Government-backed way of helping exporters. In this way, the exporters can insure against buyers failing to pay
To extrude (5) To pull into lengths
Flange (6) A projecting collar
FOB (7) Free on Board. The buyer pays all transport/insurance charges from the time the goods are put on the ship
Forwarding agent (9) Agent specializing in the transport of goods to or from a port
FTO (7) Foreign Trade Organization. The Comecon system of dealing with external trade.
GNP (2) Gross National Product
Hard currency (7) Currency which holds its value and can therefore be easily exchanged internationally—eg German marks, Swiss francs, US dollars, etc
Intensive care systems (5) Systems which keep very seriously ill patients alive by helping their heart/breathing
Letter of Credit (2) Document issued by a bank. In foreign trade, the buyer arranges for his bank to open a credit in the country of the seller.
OPEC (3) Organization of Petroleum Exporting Countries
Operating theatre (5) The room in a hospital where operations are done
Overheads (7) Costs involved in maintaining and running factories and offices—salaries, rent, heating, etc
Pellets (5) Small, regular shaped pieces
Penalty clause (7) A clause in the contract making the supplier financially responsible for late delivery
Plant (7) Fixtures and machinery used in an industrial process
PVC (5) Polyvinyl chloride, a type of plastic
Quantity discount (7) A price reduction for a very large order
Radio-opaque (5) That which shows up on an X-ray machine
Raw materials (5) The natural materials from which the product is made
Samples (7) A selection of products for demonstration
Share capital (2) The total of shares issued by a company. This is usually shown under various categories on the balance sheet.
To sterilize (5) To kill all germs/bacteria
Stethoscope (1) An instrument for listening to the heart beat and breathing
Sticking plaster (1) A strip of cloth which is put over small cuts in the skin
Straightforward transit (9) Through journey with no problems
Surgeon (1) The doctor with the knife!
To switch cargoes (9) To change orders from one consignee to another
Syringe (10) A device for giving injections
Trade embargoes (7) When it is forbidden to trade with certain countries
Trial order (7) A small first order to see how good the supplies are
To weld (6) To join together by heat